Physical Expression on Stage and Screen

Using the Alexander Technique to Create Unforgettable Performances

BILL CONNINGTON

B L O O M S B U R Y

LONDON · NEW DELHI · NEW YORK · SYDNEY

Bloomsbury Methuen Drama
An imprint of Bloomsbury Publishing Plc

50 Bedford Square	1385 Broadway
London	New York
WC1B 3DP	NY 10018
UK	USA

www.bloomsbury.com

Bloomsbury is a registered trade mark of Bloomsbury Publishing Plc

First published 2014

© Bill Connington, 2014

British Library Cataloguing-in-Publication Data
A catalogue record for this book is available from the British Library.

ISBN: PB: 978-1-4081-8264-2
ePDF: 978-1-4081-8265-9
ePub: 978-1-4081-8266-6

Library of Congress Cataloging-in-Publication Data
A catalog record for this book is available from the Library of Congress.

Typeset by Integra Software Services Pvt. Ltd.
Printed and bound in India

Physical Expression on Stage and Screen

"*Physical Expression on Stage and Screen* is a clear, detailed, and practical account of how the Alexander Technique can help liberate performers from habitual psychophysical tensions, allowing them to access the deepest and most creative impulses in their work. Bill is a generous, openhearted, and centered presence in the classroom. Any performing artist who is serious about finding a greater sense of freedom and flow would do well to take advantage of the expertise Bill offers in this book."

WALTON WILSON, *Chair, Department of Acting, and Head of Voice and Speech, Yale School of Drama*

"In *Physical Expression on Stage and Screen*, Bill Connington brings his expertise and passion as an actor and a highly experienced teacher of the Alexander Technique to the page. The book offers a practical way of working on oneself through movement, breath, voice, imagination, and choice. In small, doable steps, Bill guides the actor toward a healthy, creative life as a performer—always with a supportive, encouraging tone and attention to process as opposed to results."

KIM JESSOR, *faculty, Tisch School of the Arts at the New York University Graduate Acting Program*

"Bill Connington writes with insight, clarity, and flair about a subject he loves and shares his valuable perspective on the training of actors by exploring the all-important connection between body, mind, and spirit. In a voice both friendly and knowledgeable, *Physical Expression on Stage and Screen* guides the actor from class to rehearsal to performance."

JESSICA WOLF, *Assistant Professor, Yale School of Drama; director of* Jessica Wolf's Art of Breathing

"Bill Connington is by far the most brilliant Alexander Technique teacher with whom I have had the privilege of working. Studying with him has been one of the great gifts of my artistic life. *Physical Expression on Stage and Screen* is a must for anyone seriously aspiring to be a performing artist as well professionals who want to continue to hone their craft."

RUTH FALCON, *faculty, Mannes School of Music; adjunct faculty, the Curtis Institute of Music; former Metropolitan Opera soprano*

"Bill Connington has deep and rich experience both as a teacher of the Alexander Technique and as an actor. He speaks from the inside and writes from the heart. His book is a must for every actor who wants to increase the depth and resonance of her work."

JANE KOMINSKY, *dance faculty and former drama faculty, the Juilliard School*

"*Physical Expression on Stage and Screen* will inspire performers of every kind to unlock the originality and natural talent inside them. Actors face daunting roadblocks—both in the world and inside themselves—and Bill's methods show them what it means to leave fear behind and do, fully, what they were born to do."

BARBARA SHER, New York Times *bestselling author of* Wishcraft *and* I Could Do Anything If I Just Knew What It Was

"*Physical Expression on Stage and Screen* presents the life-changing principles of the Alexander Technique in a fresh and accessible format. It's a must-read for actors, singers, and teachers who seek an authentic and organic approach to life and the craft of performance."

RUTH GOLDEN, *Professor of Music, Director of Vocal Studies, Long Island University, C. W. Post Campus; Metropolitan Opera audition judge*

"*Physical Expression on Stage and Screen* will take the actor on a journey of self-discovery and investigation essential to the development of skill and artistry. Bill speaks from the depth of his own experiential integration of acting and the Alexander Technique and has a rare ability to render the elusive and intangible accessible through words and exercises. This book gets to the heart of the matter."

CAROLYN SEROTA, *drama faculty, the Juilliard School*

"Although *Physical Expression on Stage and Screen* is written for actors, it also is useful for musicians, dancers, athletes, and anyone else who wishes to occupy her own skin in a way that feels more natural, with less tension and more confidence and poise. Filled with simple exercises and valuable insights, it introduces the fundamentals of Alexander Technique to those who are new to it and reinforces its central concepts for those who already practice it. It has earned a place in my studio alongside my most valued references."

JENNY CLINE, *professional flutist; Assistant Secretary, National Flute Association*

"*Physical Expression on Stage and Screen* brings a moment-to-moment practicality to what has often been presented as an abstract concept. Using easy-to-understand language, it helps any actor not only improve his or her craft but also identify ingrained habits. In that way, this book becomes a life manual. It holds the potential of bringing about positive change and a whole new way of integrating oneself as well as engaging fully with others."

LEANN OVERTON, *faculty, Manhattan School of Music; production staff, Metropolitan Opera*

For Barbara Clark
Friend, colleague, and agent,
for gently, politely, and persistently suggesting that
this book might be helpful to people

For Lauren Schiff
Friend, colleague, and master teacher,
who pointed me in the right direction

For James Lipton
Dean emeritus of the Actors Studio Drama School,
who hired me to teach the Alexander Technique there
and was very supportive of the technique and my work

And for Joyce Carol Oates
A brilliant and galvanizing collaborator
who gave me the most exciting professional
opportunities I've had so far,
with many thanks for her generosity

Contents

A Note on the Exercises

To help you understand how to do some of the core exercises in this book, I have demonstrated them in fifteen videos. They are available for you to watch, free of charge, at www.vimeo.com/channels/connington.

These videos will aid you in understanding my exploratory approach to the Alexander Technique. They are not meant to be followed as a strict protocol. All the exercises in the book are aimed at helping you to use yourself with increased freedom and ease, resulting in improved performance.

A full list of these exercises is available on page 187.

Introduction

*For as long as I can remember, the thing that gave me a
sense of wonderment, of renewal, ... [has] always been
the work of other actors.*

DANIEL DAY-LEWIS

You are an actor. Actors act. Your acting impulses are completely unique.
No one else experiences life quite the way you do. It's your task to bring
your intelligence, sensitivity, humor, sexuality and sensuality, and emotions—
all of who you are—to your work. Your body and voice are the channels for
your feelings, thoughts, intuition, and instincts: they allow you to reveal *who
you are.* That's what the audience wants to know; that's why audiences attend
theater and film, to see stories brought truthfully to life—by you. You integrate
who you are into the character you are playing: the two of you merge together,
and that results in the transformational moment that the audience experiences
as your "performance."

Who you are at your core—the key element that makes you special and
different from every other human being—is what I call your *essence.* On the
most superficial level, your essence is made up of things like your height, hair
color, eye color, and body type. But beyond the initial impression that these
attributes create, there are other ingredients that are an even more essential
part of you: the range, sound, tone, and rhythm of your voice, your speech, the
words you choose to use, the way you use your body: how you stand, sit, walk,
move, and gesticulate—all give people clues about you. Even deeper still is a
sense of your personality, or what used to be called your "character"—your
deepest thoughts, feelings, and beliefs, which can be conveyed quickly, just
by someone looking at you and "getting a sense of you."

When you are in tune with yourself, people will get a sense of you quickly,
without your saying a word. You convey what is essential simply by "being."
When you are deeply connected to your essence, and divulge it consciously
to the audience, through allowing your authentic emotions out naturally, your
acting work will be compelling, specific, convincing, creative, and exciting.
Staying consistently connected to your essence will enable you to fulfill your
unique artistry.

This book aims to help you connect to that profound, essential part of yourself that every actor wants to share with an audience. It's my task to help you unlock your original and particular talent and to help you let it fly. The most effective way to allow this to happen is to remove the barriers that block your authentic expression. These impediments come in many guises and forms, but they all spring from the same source: *tension*. This book will help you free yourself from the burden of tension and its attendant ills, so that you can organically develop your full acting potential.

Performance situations are often fraught with tension and anxiety. There can be many situations that cause worry in the performer: not enough rehearsal time, concern about a role you're not sure you can perform at your best, a "press night" that many critics will attend, and so on. All performers, even movie stars, are in a vulnerable position. They are constantly being judged by agents, casting directors, producers, their fellow actors, and the general public.

It's difficult to keep everything in perspective and stay calm in the middle of the "controlled chaos" that is a theatrical rehearsal period, or the shooting of a short film or an independent feature. A life in the performing arts is full of competition, hard work, nagging doubts, and making your own way. In a certain sense it's much more complex than having a conventional full-time job in an office or institution, and such pressure can naturally sometimes lead to crippling mental-emotional-physical tension. It happens often, and it's understandable.

Tension is frequently sparked by something outside yourself, the *stressor*, that results in something created within yourself, the *stress*. We can even unintentionally be our own stressor, through ingrained thought patterns ("Why do I always mess up, every time?"). Tension can start in your mind ("That other guy is going to get the part over me, I just know it"), your emotions ("I hate the musical director because he hates my voice"), or in your body ("My back is so tight, I'll never be able to hit that high note"). But no matter where it originates, tension quickly spreads and affects the other parts of you because you are a three-part system—*mind-body-emotions*. All three of these elements are inextricably interconnected: they are all part of your instrument. They are all part of you.

One of the most important things you'll learn from this book is how to get these three components of yourself working together in harmony. When you allow that to happen, you'll be well on your way to performing stress-free. Although some teachers say you must learn to "use" your tension, I've never heard anyone explain or demonstrate how to do that effectively. Ironically, our own issues may not even be on our personal radar, even though they may be crystal clear to others observing us. It's always

. easier to see other people's habits than our own. Tension can appear as a tight neck, tense, rounded shoulders, a slumped or overarched back, stilted, awkward, or loping movement, overall stiffness in the body, and uncomfortable gestures.

That's where this book comes in. If you're ever not certain of what to do with your hands or how to make a meaningful gesture, or if your movement feels fine in daily life, and you barely notice it—but then you suddenly become self-conscious about your body and movement when onstage, or in front of a camera, this book is here to help.

The same goes for your voice. You may feel your voice and speech are fine when talking with your friends and family, talking on the phone, and asking questions in the classroom. But standing on a stage, you might feel your throat tighten, your jaw get stiff, and your voice become difficult to carry. Your everyday speech may feel casual, comfortable, and perfectly natural, but when confronted with a printed text in front of you, you suddenly feel unnatural and awkward. Restriction can result in a tight tongue and jaw, a closed throat, a stiff rib cage and diaphragm, and a lack of flexibility in the vocal mechanism, which can make you breathe shallowly or even lead you to hold your breath. This behavior sometimes results in a voice that is strained, raspy, abrupt-sounding, or overly breathy. At the other extreme, the voice can be too nasal, flat, and uncommunicative. This book is here to help with that, too.

Perhaps most critical for the performer are the mental-emotional challenges resulting from tension and stress. Emotions are the most basic material of your acting performances: they are what you want to communicate in your desire to "live the part." That's why most actors become actors. Yet somehow it can be a struggle to connect easily and deeply with your feelings, wants, and desires—the very things you're trying to share with the audience. Tension can lead to making you feel insecure, which can make you feel imbalanced, lacking in confidence, and even distrustful of your emotions. Generalized anxiety about even just being in the profession can manifest in innumerable ways. It can lead to avoiding working on your craft or going to class for fear you won't do well. Concern about fulfilling the requirements of a certain role can grip you, and this makes it difficult to come to terms with a character in a direct and effective way. It can even affect you in such a basic way that makes it difficult to learn your lines.

Anxiety can also make it almost impossible to find the quiet, focused concentration which is vital for working on creating a character. Apprehension can lead you into pushing too hard for results in your acting as you attempt to build a performance. Some acting teachers call this *indicating*, which means mimicking a character's outward behavior without connecting deeply with his or her thoughts and feelings. This type of performance can come across as shallow or hollow. In some cases tension can lead to *stage fright* or *performance anxiety*, or even a panic attack, where you choke and it becomes difficult to function.

You might be thinking, "Isn't lots of adrenaline good for you—doesn't that feed your performances?" Only partly. Tension can make you afraid to take risks. It can make it difficult for you to think clearly and perform the complex tasks every actor is asked to perform. In short, tension stops you doing what you need to do. It can even make you lose touch temporarily with "who you are"—your essence—which every performer needs to stay in touch with in order to play a role effectively and truthfully. So what's an actor to do?

My solution, when I was first starting out in the field, was to try the Alexander Technique. I found that it showed me how to do everything more easily and more naturally—breathe more freely and speak more fluidly and fluently. Move more lightly and gracefully. And perform at my best possible level.

All of the principles in this book are based on the Alexander Technique. That's because, in addition to being a working actor, I'm a certified teacher of the technique. I discovered the method while I was at drama school, and it was the most important thing I learned while I was there. It helped me improve how I use my mind, body, and voice, helped rid me of severe back pain and the emotional pressure I put on myself, all of which got in the way of my acting. Later, when I was teaching at the Actors Studio Drama School, I used the Alexander Technique, and its basic principles, to create a unique system of mind-body exercises that are the basis of this book.

The fundamental Alexander principles are sensory awareness (awareness of yourself through your mind-body and senses), inhibition (stopping of old, unconstructive habits), direction (process instructions to develop new, constructive habits), and constructive conscious control (positive management of yourself).

F. M. Alexander, the inventor of the technique, was born in the nineteenth century, so some of his language is slightly archaic. I have equated each of his principles with more contemporary words we can all understand easily:

Sensory Awareness—Sense
Inhibition—Poise
Direction—Flow
Constructive Conscious Control—Choice

I'll go into each of these concepts in depth in the first few chapters. At this juncture, it's enough to say that these four concepts will aid in taking you in a new direction, in allowing you to see yourself as a totality, an integrated whole, as opposed to a series of separate parts. If you work with the four concepts, you'll see how all your body parts—the muscles that relate to how you use your body in movement, the parts that relate to voice and speech, and the different intellectual and emotional aspects of yourself—can work together as a harmonious unity. The mind does not have to be in conflict with the body. They can cooperate and work together; they are part of the same continuum. One of the greatest acting authorities of the twentieth century, Laurence Olivier, spoke to this issue quite elegantly. In the 1960s, when it was uncommon for an English gentleman to spend time lifting weights at the gym, a reporter asked Olivier why he worked out. Olivier answered, "Because the body is sovereign to the voice." He might have answered, "The body is sovereign to the voice-breath-thought-emotions-humanity."

Try repeating these words to yourself: "Sense. Poise. Flow. Choice."

If you do this a few times each day, for a week, you will start to experience the beginnings of a subtle yet radical shift within yourself. You will begin to understand and feel, viscerally, not only the possibility but also the necessity and inevitability of mind-body transformation within yourself. Let's go on that journey together.

PART ONE

Preparing Yourself

1

The Alexander Technique and Theater Training

The Alexander Technique is a mind-body method for learning how to identify and change the mental-physical habits that cause stress, tension, misalignment, and pain. Through practicing the technique, you learn how to be more aware of what's happening in your body and in your movement, how to prevent the mental and physical misuse of yourself that creates your tension, and how to develop more positive, constructive ways of thinking and using your entire psycho-physical being. With the study of the Alexander Technique, students report that they feel lighter and easier in their bodies, calmer, and more confident. In reducing unnecessary strain, there comes a greater sense of awareness, a readiness to act, deeper, easier breathing, a more open, resonant voice, enhanced focus, and improvement in overall performance. Not bad! That's what every actor is looking for.

Sometimes actors say, "The Alexander Technique is the same as yoga and Pilates, isn't it?" It's a little like saying North Carolina and Tennessee are the same state. North Carolina and Tennessee are both states in America, and are even adjacent, but they are not the same state. The Alexander Technique is not a system of muscular exercises, as Pilates is. Nor is it like yoga—a series of physical postures.

Rather, the Alexander Technique is about building awareness of your own body and changing unconstructive physical habits. You can practice it anywhere at any time. You don't need to wear special clothing, you don't need a mat, and you don't have to put aside an hour in a gym to practice it. You can think about it where you want, when you want, for as long as you like. After you gain some experience in the method, even just thinking about it for a few minutes can help create measurable positive changes. Much more than a fitness program or a series of targeted exercises, the Alexander Technique is an approach to life.

It is important to note that the Alexander Technique is also a hands-on method. In addition to studying the ideas, concepts, and exercises in this book, I highly recommend that every actor study with a certified Alexander teacher. So much is learned through the teacher's touch and the individual attention she gives. Whether in private lessons or group classes, a certified instructor uses subtle and highly skilled hands-on work, as well as verbal instruction, to help guide a student through gentle movements, both upright and lying down. Everything the teacher does is individualized for you and what you need. The instructor can pinpoint physical habits you may have that aren't constructive and show you more beneficial ways of sitting, standing, bending, reaching, and other everyday movements.

The teacher may also apply the Alexander Technique to your acting work. You might perform some of your acting speeches for her, or sing during your lesson. You may bring in an acting partner and the teacher can coach the two of you in what you are doing physically and vocally. The teacher will help you apply the Alexander ideas while you are actually practicing your craft. I found the Alexander Technique to be one of the greatest acting tools I have ever come across.

While an Alexander teacher is an objective, informed outside source who can help you tremendously in your growth as an actor, gradually you will learn to become your own best teacher, because you are with yourself all the time. You learn to catch yourself in the act of tightening up—or, even better, before you tighten up—and you coach yourself into new, positive ways of doing things. For instance, instead of learning your lines hunched up on your bed, with your shoulders up around your ears, you may find other more comfortable ways of learning your lines that are easier on your body. If you're a person intimidated by singing, instead of your throat closing before another dreaded singing lesson, you can learn ways to release your mind-body beforehand and carry that freedom into your performance.

I see the Alexander Technique as a fundamental building block of your acting technique because it familiarizes you with yourself. After all, to transform yourself into someone else, it's essential to know the materials you're starting with: you. Before you can successfully take on the extreme physicality of a role like Richard III, for example, it's necessary to know where your own calm, poised, and at-center "neutral" is. Otherwise, each character you develop is destined from the start to share at least some of the same traits that spring from the pool of your own unintentional personal habits.

I want to go into more specifics about the Alexander Technique and how I got involved with it, but first I'll let you know something about Mr. Alexander himself. Since he was an actor, director, and a producer, some of the issues that affected him might also affect you.

F. M. Alexander's Story

F. M. (Frederick Matthias) Alexander was born in Tasmania, a large island off the coast of Australia, in 1869. He grew up on a small farm in a remote area. The family owned horses, and Alexander had a lifelong love of riding. He lived daily with these highly trained and coordinated animals. His close observation of the animals later influenced how he came to observe himself and other people. Starting when he was an adolescent, Alexander studied acting and reciting. It was common during that period to have "parlor performances," in which amateur and professional performers would sing or recite selections from Shakespeare and poetry in homes, community centers, or small theaters. Alexander became known locally for his high-quality recitals.

As a young man in his early twenties, he lived in both Melbourne and Sydney, continuing his acting studies, performing his recitals, acting in plays, and supplementing his income with office work. He then turned professional, started his own acting company, which toured Australia, and also founded one of the first modern drama schools. This was one of the first performing arts conservatories to have what is now considered to be the standard curriculum: instruction in acting, voice, speech, movement, dance, fencing, stage combat, and other related subjects. Until this point, most actors learned their craft piecemeal—through private coaching and "on the job" in theater companies, watching and learning from more experienced professionals. In this, as in many things, Alexander was extremely innovative and groundbreaking.

Just as Alexander's acting career was gaining more ground, he developed a problem that got in the way of his performances and almost stopped his acting career cold. When he was acting he would often become hoarse, sometimes seriously so. His colleagues reported to him that he was gasping audibly for air when he inhaled, and this distracted from his performances. This distressed Alexander, since he was a very hard worker, almost fastidious in his approach—in short, he wanted very badly to "do it right." He later came to understand that it was this very impulse to "get it right" that was instrumental in creating his own problem.

Before he made that discovery, he first tried to get help from medical doctors and voice teachers. The doctors saw that there was nothing organically wrong with Alexander's throat or vocal mechanism, and so suggested vocal rest for two weeks. After resting his voice, the hoarseness would disappear. But then it would come back again when he resumed performing. Alexander repeated this process several times. He had one particularly important performance, during which he actually lost his voice. Discouraged, he visited his doctor again. Alexander was convinced that vocal rest alone was not taking care of the unknown underlying condition. Since there was nothing wrong with him physically, he asked the doctor if it was possible that something he was *doing with himself might be the cause of the problem*. The doctor agreed that this must be the case; however, he was at a loss to identify what Alexander was doing incorrectly.

Alexander's Discovery

Using his remarkable powers of observation and unusual persistence, Alexander studied himself in three-way mirrors while performing everyday movements such as standing, sitting, raising an arm, and taking a step. He also studied himself while reciting. He noticed a number of things: when he began to speak, *he pulled his head back and down, which put pressure down onto his neck and throat.* This was the cause of his vocal problems: he was constricting his throat with tension. The compression of his head onto his neck created downward pressure throughout his whole body, causing a chain reaction of tension down through his spine and torso.

He also noticed that when he recited he lifted his shoulders, arched his lower back, and stiffened his legs. These problems were also indirectly related to the retraction of his head pulling down onto his spine. Even when he wasn't reciting, he saw that the habits he had in performance were evident in his everyday life, though in less pronounced form.

Watching himself in the mirror, Alexander saw that he initiated *all* movement by pressing his head back and down. He also learned that he was unable to stop his gasping or improve his breathing or speaking *directly*. He needed to approach the problem *indirectly*. When he was able to balance his head at the top of his spine in a poised fashion, this removed the compression throughout his body, which indirectly stopped the hoarseness and loss of voice. It took many months of observation, experimentation, and trial and error to begin to change his way of being.

Alexander noticed many positive changes in himself as a result of his work. When his head was poised, he achieved *optimal spinal lengthening*. There was a natural broadening of his shoulders when he stopped lifting them up. Overall there was much less tension throughout his whole body. He became more familiar with his own thinking process and his tendency to push for results, especially when reciting. He saw that, in addition to purely physical and vocal changes, he needed to change certain basic mental concepts in order to facilitate the change in himself.

I cannot stress enough how radical Alexander's work was at the time. In our time, we take for granted that the mind and body are connected. Everyone understands that mental stress can result in physical stress and vice versa. But in the 1890s, this was not at all understood in the Western world. The mind was considered superior to the body. There was almost no information on what we would now call mind-body modalities, or complementary, alternative, or integrative medicine—this all lay far in the future. This made Alexander's discoveries all the more remarkable.

Alexander eradicated his own vocal problems over the course of a number of years, all while pursuing his acting career and running his acting company and school. His voice gave him no more problems, and he thought that his period of intensive self-study was over. But other actors with vocal problems soon began appealing to him for help. Then public speakers started appearing at his door. Doctors became aware of his work and sent him patients with breathing problems, such as asthma. Alexander became known as the Breathing Man.

By 1904, money was raised to relocate Alexander to London so he could bring his work to a wider audience. He set up his practice in central London and taught his technique to many well-known actors of the day, including Lillie Langtry, Sir Henry Irving, and, later, the film star Leslie Howard, among many others. His practice expanded to help those with other issues, such as neck and back pain, poor posture, and performance anxiety. He worked with the famous scientist Sir Charles Sherrington, the father of modern neurology; the archbishop of Canterbury, William Temple; statesman Sir Stafford Cripps; and eminent intellectuals Aldous Huxley, John Dewey, and George Bernard Shaw. Alexander worked full time until his death, at the age of eighty-six, in 1955. He left behind a number of qualified teachers to continue his work, and the influence of the technique has continued to grow with each decade since his passing.

My Theater Training

I discovered the Alexander Technique while I was training as an actor in England. I attended the London Academy of Music and Dramatic Art, where voice and movement training were highly emphasized. We were immersed in the great plays of the past—versatility was stressed to enable us to play a large range of characters and to perform all periods and styles authentically.

It was a thrilling time: taking classes all day and rehearsing plays in the evening. There was barely time to get home at night, learn lines, and show up first thing in the morning to start all over again. On the weekends, and on the few evenings when there wasn't a rehearsal, we would go to the theater.

Most of the acting students at LAMDA were English, but there were students from all over the world. There were many talented young people, speaking with all kinds of accents, working hard at their craft. One never knew what would happen next. It was a vital, energetic, stimulating time. I loved it. And I was very, very tense.

While most of this activity was positive, I was trying much too hard to do everything "right." This was the same fundamental problem that Alexander had. I was the proverbial "good student." This resulted in a tight and overarched lower back, hunched shoulders, a caved-in chest, and a pushed-forward neck that put pressure on my throat, constricted my breathing, and restricted my speaking voice. I leaned forward onto my toes. My body attitude was, "Whatever you want—I can do it, and fast!" I was nineteen years old, and I was suffering from bad back pain. The school sent me to a doctor, who took X-rays. He told me there was nothing physically wrong with my spine or my back muscles themselves. The diagnosis was extreme tension in my back.

Luckily, an Alexander Technique teacher was hired at the school, right after my diagnosis. Her name was Glynn MacDonald. In our weekly work together, she showed me how I was putting unnecessary pressure on myself—physically, vocally, and mentally. Her approach was gentle, constructive, indirect rather than overly prescriptive, encouraging, creative, and quietly inspirational. Somehow, this subtle, hands-on class that dealt with my "whole self" became the most important class in the school for me. While the other classes were beneficial and instructive, they all dealt with "parts" of me— voice, speech, movement, and other individual aspects. Here was a class that helped me see that I was a totality. And that I could work as a balanced and coordinated whole.

I experienced the beneficial effects of the Alexander work immediately. I felt the weight being lifted off my shoulders—psycho-physically. My body felt lighter, freer, more flexible, more comfortable. Most important, I felt calmer, more centered, more in control of my own thoughts and body. *My introduction to the Alexander work profoundly changed how I approach my acting work.* I understood, for the first time, that if I could stay balanced within my self, I would be composed and focused. I could approach my work in a methodical and constructive way, work under extreme conditions, sometimes with challenging people, and I could still deliver my best work.

Studying the Alexander Technique made my back pain go away, because I learned how to change *how I used myself.* My breathing improved—it became deeper and more free-flowing. I felt much more relaxed in daily life and in classes and rehearsals. I stopped worrying so much about what I was doing and just did it.

I returned to America, moved to New York, and started to work in the theater. The Alexander Technique helped me stay focused as I auditioned, met with casting directors, and "pounded the pavement." It helped me stay steady and on an even keel when living in a bustling, crowded, intense city in a challenging, overcrowded profession. It also helped me be bold in my acting choices when auditioning and performing. I felt inspired to try things out, was willing to make mistakes, and to not be too careful. This was invaluable to me in my growth as a performer.

But I was still working too hard. I remember being on a bus that was stuck in clogged traffic. I wasn't late. I had plenty of time to get where I was going. But my whole body was leaning forward. Subconsciously, I was trying to help the bus move forward! I realized that I needed to do much more work on myself. I knew what had helped me the most in my studies in England was the Alexander Technique. Now it was time to study the technique in New York.

I found a highly qualified teacher: Barbara Kent. She understood the pressures performers are under; she was a performer herself. Barbara trained as a classical singer at the Juilliard School and taught voice and the Alexander Technique. I studied with Barbara for a year and a half while I was auditioning and acting. After that time, I decided to train as an Alexander teacher myself to deepen my understanding of the method and myself, to give myself invaluable help as an actor, and to learn how to teach the technique to others. It was exciting to combine my two passions: acting and the Alexander Technique. The three-year Alexander training passed by in a flash.

The Actors Studio Drama School

One of the most fruitful teaching assignments I've had was at the Actors Studio MFA Program. I was hired by Dean James Lipton, the host of the famous *Inside the Actors Studio* program on Bravo. Dean Lipton, along with other leaders at the Actors Studio, helped to develop a three-year MFA program based on the techniques used by members of the Studio, especially the deeply personal acting approach labeled by others as "method acting." This approach is based on the teachings of the turn-of-the-twentieth-century Russian actor-director-theorist Constantin Stanislavski, who sought to discover the difference between the standard acting of his time, which seemed false to him, with its series of clichéd gestures, movements, and indicated emotions, and the performances by great artists that seemed real and transcendent.

I was hired as the Alexander teacher soon after the MFA program was formed. The Alexander classes I designed for the students there were unlike any class I had taught before. I gathered information about the program from Dean Lipton, his assistants, and the school's acting faculty. I observed acting classes with many different teachers so I could have a sense of how others were working. I experimented a great deal with my students in the classroom to find what worked for them and the program. I wanted the Alexander classes to complement what was happening in the rest of the program.

While there are many ways to teach movement and Alexander Technique for actors, I wanted to streamline my approach to make sure that everything—all acting choices and impulses, including the use of the body and movement—originated from *emotional motivations* as opposed to being imposed by me from the outside. This approach often results in work that is unique, surprising, and unexpected. I wanted my approach to be organic, nonjudgmental, and open. It was fun and challenging to work in this way.

I've also worked with more "classical" approaches to acting, including some in which movement forms are "choreographed" on the actors' bodies. Work with masks and much "period work"—plays that take place in the past, such as the work of Shakespeare and the Restoration comedies—are often dealt with in this choreographed way. But all good actors are looking for the same thing: an authentic and convincing performance, so that the audience "suspends disbelief" and accepts you as the character you are playing. Whatever the genre, the actor must find her way into making the movement her own and finding its emotional impulse.

My time at the Actors Studio MFA Program was very stimulating, and in that creative environment I developed many of the approaches and exercises that are in this book. We did physical warm-ups that included centering, stretching, gentle strengthening, and rhythmic exercises. We explored the various body parts, such as the neck, shoulders, torso, and hips. We covered how they are structured, how they relate to other parts of the body, how they balance, and how they move. I helped students find freedom and flexibility in various activities, such as walking, running, sitting, bending, jumping, reaching, moving while making sound, and observing physical habits during movement. There was also floor work; the students learned many techniques for releasing the body that they could practice at home. In the last ten minutes of the class, I worked with an individual student in a private session on whatever she needed.

The classes were based on the following principles:

- Expansion versus contraction
- Spontaneity versus stopping yourself
- Sensation versus numbness
- Courage and availability versus fear
- Openness versus closing down
- Acceptance versus being overly critical
- Balance versus holding still
- Flow versus jerk and hold
- Having a sense of the space around you
- Having a sense of yourself in relation to the people around you
- Feeling the flow of emotions in relation to the flow of the body

- Exploring versus knowing
- Taking your time
- Process versus results
- Understanding that you are beginning a lifelong study of yourself

Following are some simple exercises that you can try anytime, anywhere. After the first exercise, you'll need a notebook and pen, laptop, or your phone to do some writing. There are many benefits to beginning with simple exercises. First, it's easier to remember them. Second, if the exercises are simple and don't take much time, you will actually do them. As you work your way through this book, you can mark the exercises that are most helpful to you and put together a personal routine. *Your personal routine will only take you a few minutes a day.* Find small pockets of time when you can work on yourself productively, such as:

- As soon as you get up in the morning
- Right before you go to bed at night
- At the beginning or end of your lunch period, or on a break at work
- Sitting in traffic
- Walking down the street, standing, or waiting for the traffic light to change
- During a break from being online or watching television

Finding Where You Are

Sit in a comfortable chair. Think of being easily at your full height—meaning without slumping but without being ramrod straight. Have your feet on the floor, your hands in your lap. Leave your eyes open. Be aware of the room and what's in it, including the sounds inside and outside the room.

Tune into your breathing—see if you can sense it going in and out. Take note if it seems to be shallow or if you're holding your breath.

Scan yourself from head to toe—what are you aware of in your muscles, in your body? If you feel any tension, note where it is.

Give yourself the suggestion to let your breath slow down and be easy—don't force it. *Let it be a thought your body responds to.*

Suggest to yourself that all your muscles be easy.

Sit quietly, giving your attention to freeing your muscles and to your breath flowing in and out. Observe yourself in this way for three minutes or so.

Know that this is where you are. The more you practice this, the more "centered" you will become. And this centeredness will become your "new normal." This is the ideal place from which to act.

Mind-Body Journal

Get your notebook and pen, laptop, or phone. You're about to start your mind-body journal. Without thinking too much about it, write everything that crossed your mind during the "Finding Out Where You Are" exercise: what you were thinking, what you were feeling, what you noticed about the room, what you noticed about yourself. If the answer is "I didn't notice much," dig a little deeper. Were you hot or cold? Did you notice any tension in your body, and if so, where? Was it sharp, dull, faint, or very present? Any aches anywhere? Were there any parts of your body that were uncomfortable? Did any part of you feel numb or hard to be aware of? What did you notice about your breathing throughout the exercise? Did it change at all during the exercise? Did giving yourself the instruction to release your muscles have any effect on your body and breath?

Let's call this first entry in your journal home base. This is where you're starting. It's good to remember, so that you can compare later on and use it as a signpost. I suggest that you take a few minutes each day, perhaps at the beginning or the end of the day, when it's quiet, to write in your mind-body journal. If you commit to keeping a journal, it will become a fundamental part of unlocking psycho-physical blocks that might be holding you back.

Coming Down onto the Floor

If squatting is not comfortable for you, you can kneel down, come onto your haunches, and get down onto the floor from there. It's often best to avoid doing a reverse sit-up as you lie down. Most people can't do that without overtensing in the neck and shoulders. Coming down onto your side and then rolling over onto your back avoids that issue. This is also a constructive way to get into bed. The main objective is to maintain your lengthening throughout the movement, leave your body as free as possible, and keep breathing.

- Stand with your feet comfortably apart.
- Think an easy upward flow through your torso.
- As you think up, bend your knees forward and lean forward from your hips.
- Come all the way down into a squat.
- If you need to, hold onto a chair on the way down.
- Sit on the floor or a mat.

- Come onto your side, as you slide one arm above your head along the floor, and your legs straighten in the opposite direction.
- Roll over onto your back.
- Remind yourself that these kinds of transitional movements are an important part of your acting process.

Constructive Rest

The phrase *constructive rest* refers to the position of lying on the floor, with support under your head, and your knees bent. A natural way of releasing the body and the mind, the position encourages a natural, easy flow of air.

A firm but not too hard support works best for your headrest—a paperback book or a thin towel folded several times. If you don't have something under your head, it will retract back and down, putting a strain on the base of your skull and down onto your neck and shoulders. Make sure the support is high enough to be comfortable for you. Usually a book anywhere between three quarters of an inch and three inches will work, depending on your size and anatomy. When you rest your hands on your lower rib cage, it helps to encourage your shoulders and chest to open.

- Lie on your back on a carpeted floor or exercise mat.
- Place a paperback book underneath your head for support.
- Bend your knees and place your feet on the floor, about hip width apart.
- If your back hurts, or you have an arched back, place your lower legs on a chair to support them. Gravity will help your lower back to naturally fall back toward the floor.
- Put your hands on your lower rib cage to have a sense of your own breathing.
- Allow your body to be supported by the floor. Be aware of yourself against the floor and in space.
- Pay attention to your breathing. Is it fast or slow? Even or uneven? Is one part of your rib cage moving more than another? Take in this information without judging yourself.
- Scan your body from head to toe. Are you aware of tension or stiffness anywhere? If so, make a mental note of it.
- Allow yourself to be aware of your thoughts, as well as your body. If your mind wanders, gently bring yourself back to your mind-body. Stay easily focused on your breathing, and yourself.

- Stay in this position for five to ten minutes.
- Acknowledge the luxury of giving yourself this time to be with yourself.
- Try to make this a daily practice. You deserve it.

Getting Up off the Floor

This is a movement that most people don't think much about, but it can lead to a great deal of tightening when performed in a habitual way. It's useful when getting up in the morning as well. When you get out of bed, roll onto your side rather than doing a sit-up. It puts much less pressure on your neck, shoulders, and back.

- Roll from your back onto your side.
- Use your hands to help propel you into a sitting position.
- Allow your neck, shoulders, and back to remain easy as you come into the sitting position.
- Give yourself a moment to readjust to a different position.
- Come into a squatting position, then come up into standing position.
- Alternatively, kneel on one knee, putting the other foot in front. Rise into a standing position.
- Allow your whole body, especially your neck and lower back, to stay easy as you rise.
- Let your body be a single integrated unit as you stand.
- Note how you feel different in your mind-body.
- Take a few steps and notice how your movement is after this period of self-reflection.

The Primary Exercise—Sitting

All day long we engage in innumerable activities. We are *doing* all the time. What happens if we *stop doing*? All you need for this exercise is a chair and a few minutes. You can go through it on the bus or subway, or driving a car. Try it sitting in a doctor's office, or taking a break from work at home. When waiting for an audition, why not follow these steps rather than speaking nervously with the person next to you? As preparation for a rehearsal, it's a useful way to quickly and efficiently clear away the distracting events of your day and bring yourself to the task at hand.

- Sit comfortably, in a relatively straight-backed chair if possible.
- Place yourself against the back of the chair, or forward on the edge of the chair. Sitting in the middle of the seat can sometimes lead to slumping.
- Put both your feet on the floor and place your hands on your lap to help keep your shoulders and chest open.
- If you need back support, place a small pillow or rolled-up sweater behind your back to help your spine stay elongated.
- Sense your body supported by the seat and back of the chair. Be aware of your feet against the floor and your body in the environment.
- Scan your body for tension.
- Allow yourself to be easily upright rather than slumped or too stiffly upright. Think up through your body, without "making it happen." *Let it be a thought, an intention.*
- What's happening with your breathing? Is it fast or slow? Even or uneven? High or low?
- Be mindful of your thoughts as well as your body. If your attention wavers, gently bring it back to your mind-body. Maintain an easy focus on your breathing and yourself.
- At the end of three minutes, see if you feel subtly different in your mind-body.
- This is what I call "dropping in." You can do it several times a day to get a sense of where you are: physically, mentally, and emotionally. Vital for any actor.

The Primary Breath Exercise—Sighing

- Lie down in the constructive rest position, or sit comfortably in a chair.
- Let your body gently be at its full stature. Stay easy: don't force it; think it. Your body will follow your intention.
- Place your hands on your lower rib cage.
- Sense your breath dropping all the way down to the bottom of your lungs, but without pushing it. Let it be an idea in your mind.
- Allow yourself to breathe in this free manner for a minute or two.
- Allow whatever breath you have to breathe out easily on a sigh. Don't take a special breath in.
- Wait for a few moments. Then sigh again. Pause. Then sigh for a third time.
- The act of sighing gently will help you release physical and emotional tension, leaving you more open for your acting work.

Mind-Body Opening

This exercise is a gentle way to begin to take mind-body freedom into movement. Reminding yourself to allow yourself to be at your full height helps to energize your body without forcing. Thinking of your legs releasing down toward the ground as your spine releases up helps to reinforce the dynamic opposition that is necessary in the human body. The drawing of your arms up and out will help to counteract the tendency to slope the shoulders forward, and for your arms to hang listlessly at your sides. These simple movements help your torso move up and out, rather than down and in. By opening yourself physically, you help to open yourself emotionally, almost to say, "Yes, I'm ready to open myself in all ways, in all directions." What a great place from which to start a rehearsal or performance!

- Stand with your feet easily apart. Ask yourself not to slump or to stand overly straight.
- Gently think up through your torso.
- Think open through your chest and shoulders. Allow your arms to hang easily at your sides.
- Be aware of your breath dropping into the bottom of your lungs.
- Sense the front, back, and sides of your body. Remember that you are three-dimensional.
- Feel your feet against the floor and your head going up toward the ceiling.
- Slowly and smoothly spread your arms out to either side, to shoulder level.
- Float your arms back to your sides.
- Gently stretch your arms out to the side a second time.
- Imagine energy coming up along your spine, through your arms, and out through your fingertips.
- Float your arms back down to your sides.
- Elongate your arms out to the sides, then up toward the ceiling, your fingertips stretching as far as they can without tightening or raising your shoulders. Repeat a second time.
- Allow your whole mind-body to open itself up—*to be ready to give and to receive*.

Mind-Body Goals

This exercise is an invaluable guidepost: you'll learn a lot from it. Put your answers somewhere safe, where you can find them easily, preferably in your mind-body journal. Check your lists every few weeks as you work your way through this book. It's an easy way of keeping you on course with your mind-body goals, but also of reminding yourself about the things you feel good about, something we can all do more often.

- Sit comfortably in a chair.
- Check in with your mind-body. How are you feeling? Where are you at the moment?
- Think up and out through your body.
- Give attention to your breathing; allow it to be easy.
- Have the intention of clearing your mind. Set aside your concerns for the moment. They will be there at the end of the exercise.
- Give three gentle sighs out.
- Sit for several moments, with a clear mind.
- Think about your body and how it may interact with your mind and your emotions. Are there ways that it functions that please you? Write those down.
- Are there things about your mind-body that you might like to change? Write those down. Take your time with both the lists.
- Try not to be overly harsh on yourself.
- Look at both lists. Is there anything you'd like to add?
- Give three more sighs.
- Let your mind be clear.
- Remind yourself that this a gradual process; you don't have to make all the changes at once.
- Be still inside and know that you can create change within yourself.

2

Sensory Awareness

Every actor makes active use of her senses. They are a critical tool in your acting equipment. Sight, hearing, taste, smell, touch: your senses not only enrich your experiences but also help you define and frame your world. They enable you to perceive yourself, others, and life around you. They help you define what is to be human.

When you touch something soft—a piece of expensive velvet, a baby's skin, a cat's newly groomed fur—the tactile experiences imprint themselves on your personal experience through your acute sense of touch and you have an emotional experience based on what you sense through your fingertips. Along with your emotions and your speech, your senses are what transmit human experience back and forth between you and the outside world.

Your sensory systems are part of your nervous system and are sophisticated channels for transmitting and translating information received in the environment and from inside yourself. Once the information from the physical world has traveled through your sensory system, it is interpreted by your brain. Your perceptions are a mental, physical, and emotional experience. These three aspects of yourself are intertwined and can't be separated. For instance, I could be standing in the middle of a busy street but immediately think of my father if I smell pipe smoke and suddenly find myself feeling a little teary because my father died young. When I smell a certain perfume, it reminds me of my mother getting ready to go out for a night on the town when I was a little boy. It pleases me to reexperience that, because my mother is still very much alive.

Some actors use the classic *sense memory*, or affective memory, exercises devised by Stanislavski and further developed by Lee Strasberg when working on their craft. The exercises lead you through actual events from your life. You remember vivid details of the events through your senses, heightened by the relaxation the exercises are devised to provoke, and this helps you to remember how you felt emotionally. Sometimes it almost feels as if you are reliving the experience. The theory is that the sense memory will help you apply the authentic feelings you experienced in the past to a scene you are performing in the present. Even if you never use classic sense memory exercises, all actors use current sensory information and remembered sensory information constantly. It's something we do naturally and instinctively. It's part of what makes you an actor.

For instance, when I teach workshops, I teach the easiest sense memory exercise there is. I ask people to walk as they normally would down the street, without thinking about it. Then I ask them to show me how they walk when they're tired. Usually people slump down more, losing some of their full height, their shoulders roll forward, and sometimes their necks jut forward. Often their walking gets a little slower. Next I ask them to show me how they walk when they are late. They walk faster, sometimes jerkier, and usually the whole body leans forward, as if this would make them get there sooner. Finally, I ask them to show me how they walk when they are both tired and late. People display a combination of the two walks.

I've taught this exercise many times, and I've never had anyone say, "I can't remember what it's like when I'm tired," or "I can't remember how I feel when I'm late." They don't realize it, but part of how they remember how they walk in those situations is through their senses. Your senses and your thinking form the basic foundation that expands your awareness of yourself.

Kinesthesia and Proprioception

I'm guessing you have quick "gut reactions" to things, are comfortable making decisions on instinct, and have feelings that spring up naturally and often. That's how most actors are. Your instinctive reactions are part of what makes you unique and unpredictable (in a good way) as a performer. Your senses inform those instincts.

Your intuition and guts come into play, but you also use a sixth sense you may not know you have called the *kinesthetic sense*. Kinesthesia allows you to be aware of your muscles, their movement, and behaviors. Through it, you interpret sensations happening inside your body. In addition, *proprioception* is a related seventh sense; it's a subtle sensory mechanism in your joints and muscles that constantly gives you information about what position and condition your body is in. It tells you how much effort is necessary to maintain a position or condition. Through it, you determine how much muscular effort seems to be needed for your everyday functioning.

Elite athletes have naturally highly developed proprioceptive and kinesthetic senses. This allows them to coordinate and use their muscles in a subtle and sophisticated fashion. But they also develop their natural talent through study and training. In that way, athletes and actors have something in common. They both get up in front of large groups of people and carry out highly complex actions that most people can only dream of. And they both need to train. It doesn't just happen—you need to practice in a productive way.

You already understand that for actors, exercise for strength, endurance, and flexibility is important, and staying in good physical condition is crucial. But the need for a deep and supple sense of balance and coordination is equally important. Proprioceptive training is common in elite athletics to help prevent injuries. For you, singing in a musical eight times a week on a steeply raked stage, or engaging in a fight scene over the course of several hours on a film set, proprioceptive training will stand you in good stead!

Specialized proprioceptive training through the Alexander Technique designed specifically for the actor helps you both consciously and subconsciously. Working with your physical agility, you can make the decision to move in a certain way, in a certain sequence, at a certain time. This is part of the actor's skill—that and the ability to repeat exactly for the camera through multiple takes or nightly on a stage.

The exercises in this book are designed to help you increase your body awareness, develop your kinesthetic and proprioceptive senses, and achieve a kind of *expanded awareness* of yourself, your environment, your acting partners, and the interrelationships between them all. But what do you do if the information you are receiving through your senses is slightly "off"? You know what to do if you have problems with your sight—you get glasses or do eye exercises to improve your vision. But what if the information from your kinesthetic and proprioceptive senses is unreliable?

Increasing your mental awareness of your proprioceptive and kinesthetic senses is a good start. As you give your attention to it, you'll begin to be more cognizant of your body in space and your movement. You'll sense how you use your body and why. You'll catch yourself in awkward positions, such as collapsing into a slump in front of the television or computer, hunching over on the exercise bicycle, or pulling your body to the side when carrying a heavy bag. Noticing these things brings a heightened awareness and a deeper realization of how you're using yourself in daily life and in your acting. You will probably find that in situations where you care the most, such as auditions, rehearsals, and performances, you may experience an increase in tension and tightness in your body, your breathing, and your emotions.

Effects of Habitual Tension on Sensory Awareness

When you use too much tension in your body, your tension can become habitual and unfelt. Sometimes you might feel that you are "doing fine" when perhaps you're not. Or you may not realize your stress levels are higher than average because you are so used to it—it feels "normal" to you. For instance, you might get stiff in the lower back, and this becomes a fixed habit. You're so conditioned to it you don't feel it, or you feel it only peripherally. Your back may get even stiffer when you are playing a big emotional scene. The stiffness can get in your way and make your movement look awkward, but more important, it may tend to block you emotionally and make it more difficult to play the scene.

When these things happen, you may have what F. M. Alexander called *unreliable sensory awareness*. It's common—almost everyone has it to some degree. But as you work to become more aware of yourself consciously and learn to release excessive tension, your senses will become more accurate.

If you compare what you *see* with what you *feel*, you may be surprised that what you see is more accurate. You may not feel imbalances, but you can objectively see if you are lifting one shoulder higher than another or if your whole body is listing to one side.

When working on improving the use of himself, Alexander became aware that what he was *feeling* and what he *observed visually* in himself were often two different things. Over time, as his kinesthetic sense became more accurate, he began to catch himself tightening, and he was gradually able to feel his own tension more clearly.

The use of his body in activity improved with time as he thought more about it. It also improved when he was not thinking about it. How you move when you're not thinking about it is what Alexander called your *standard of use*. I assure you that your standard of use gets better as you unlearn your old, inefficient habits and learn more constructive habits. I've seen it in myself.

For example, when I had private Alexander lessons with one of my mentors, Judith Leibowitz, I had the sensation that she was turning my head to the left. This was because I had a habit of twisting my head and neck to the right. When Judy positioned my head straight on the top of my spine, it felt like she was twisting and turning it to the left. As I continued to have private Alexander lessons, this feeling faded; my head got straighter, it felt more comfortable, and I had a sense of a "new normal."

In another example, a well-known Broadway singer I work with said to me, "I'm tall. When I'm in a musical, I find myself unconsciously shrinking down to be the same height as the other singer. It's like I want to be at the same level as she. I shift all my weight onto one foot and cock my head. I know this isn't a good place to sing from, but my body is used to it. It's a habit." This tightness made him feel that he was "ready to sing" when in actuality, his tension was making it harder to sing. Through working with the Alexander Technique he's no longer squeezing his vocal equipment by shrinking himself down. The results have been impressive: his voice is better than ever.

You may associate many activities with "learned tension." For instance, when you were a child you may have worried about learning to write, and so grabbed onto your pen for dear life. Or when you first learned to type on the computer, you may have been so concentrated on what you were doing that you slumped over the keys. These habits become associated with the activity, so it's hard for you to unlearn them.

Your body comes to almost believe that it's necessary to have those tensions in order to accomplish the activity. To *constructively change*, I suggest you become more aware of *how, why*, and *when* you perform your habits. You'll learn a lot, understand it better, and will be able to change them gradually.

Developing a New, Process-Oriented Approach

How exactly should you build this elusive awareness, or mindfulness, that leads to mind-body freedom? How can you not get trapped in sensory feedback that might be slightly off? After all, the number one rule for an actor is "trust your instincts" and "trust what you feel."

You will be able to more reliably trust in what you feel when you begin to shift your focus slightly. Rather than being purely results oriented, it's a matter of shifting to a more process-oriented approach. But doesn't the difficulty of getting an acting job and the need to be ready for anything necessarily lead to a results-oriented approach? Isn't it necessary for survival? To a point—but there is a fine line.

An overly goal-oriented approach is what Alexander called *end-gaining*. What he meant by that is that there is an overemphasis on the goal at the expense of the process. Pushing yourself so hard to get ahead can often lead to both physical and mental tension and stress. Being so goal oriented can lead people into thinking they are always behind, they aren't getting far enough fast enough in their careers, and the list goes on and on. These beliefs can lead to even more stress.

To counteract this negative cycle, Alexander firmly believed that if you pay attention to the process, it will naturally affect the quality of the end result in a positive way. This is a much more *process-oriented approach*. The concept of committing to the process rather than the result, and trusting that this will constructively affect the outcome, is a simple one. Yet over and over again you may catch yourself pushing for results and paying little attention to what Alexander called the *means whereby*—what we call the process.

You can see evidence of end-gaining in myriad ways: a tightened throat when performing, overemphatic gestures, lifted shoulders, hunched posture, running over a mental checklist of all the acting moments you want to "nail" in a performance, rushing through a scene "indicating" rather than living the role—it can appear in many forms. But when you pay attention to the process, both in your life and in your work, it will help keep you moving in a positive direction that is right for you.

The Open-Receptive State

The ideal state in which to lay the groundwork for a process-oriented way of functioning is what I call an *open-receptive state*. Consciously allowing your mind-body-senses to open themselves to new experiences. It's a simple concept which may not always be simple in practice. It takes repetition and trial and error. Some people find it difficult, maybe even scary. Luckily, by nature, you, as an actor, are a risk taker. You are more in touch than the average person with your mind-body-emotions, or you soon will be. You possess qualities I've heard nonperformers say they envy about actors: bravery and adaptability, being quick on your feet, and the ability to work with your whole self in a direct and striking way.

An important part of staying with the process is not pushing—mentally, physically, or emotionally. We're all used to *doing* things. In learning a new skill, most often we learn what to *do*: a series of steps, a set of actions, checking things off a list. But often in trying, we end up forcing too much. This can create unwanted tension and doesn't bring us the results we want.

Another part of the "non-doing," no-pushing approach is a willing suspension of *judgment*. Without realizing it, we are often judgmental of others, and even more so of ourselves. I urge you to stop beating yourself up and to focus on what you can bring to the character and the scene. In the Alexander Technique, there is an expression that is used: *Leave yourself alone.* It means: leave yourself in an open and receptive state. It's almost like a state of grace, and *time appears to slow down.* When you are in the moment, you can *stay with yourself.* Staying with yourself will leave you more open to all the quicksilver changes in the acting world—from inevitable changes in the business side of things to the moment-by-moment work you need to do in acting a scene.

The process-oriented way of working is not always easy to adopt if other actors around you are rushing to achieve results right away. Often it requires you to be the calm center of the storm. Acknowledge to yourself the tension and anxiety around you while committing to taking a different approach. It's important not to "take on" others' fear. In the long run, your overall progress will benefit because you will be truly open to change. Maintaining a balanced sense of yourself in the moment will help you improve the quality of whatever you are doing.

You'll be able to *catch yourself in the act of tightening* in many different ways: slouching in a chair while you're eating, walking with your shoulders sloped forward and your lower back arched, hunched over a book or your handheld device with your body in a C curve, and so on. Once you start catching yourself, you're on the way to being able to change for the better. You'll become more cognizant of how you walk up and down stairs, how you bend over to pick something up off the floor, how you fix food in the kitchen, and so on. You'll notice what you're doing in sports activities: running, riding a bike, taking a walk, taking a dance class, or working out at the gym.

Let's reword the old saying "Practice makes perfect" and make it "Process makes perfect." When you approach the exercises at the end of each chapter as a process, with confidence and patience, you will understand that working with yourself, step by step, will bring you where you want to go—on the way to creating performances you used to only imagine but can now actually realize.

Mind-Body Habits and the Startle Reflex

Habit is strong. You're used to doing things a certain way, from learning lines and singing to high-stakes emotional interactions such as working with acting partners or communicating with your agent. Your habits function on all levels: physical, mental, and emotional. Often the instigator of these mental-physical-emotional habits is the *startle reflex*.

Patterns of behavior can grow out of your fear reactions. Sometimes they are subtle, and fear can block your innate acting impulses. This manifests itself in the startle reflex, or the *fight or flight response*. This reflex is organically built into human beings to help them survive. This response can be traced back to the time when humans were primarily hunter-gathers or fighters. There were many times when men and women were in life-threatening situations. It was then necessary to either stand your ground and fight the enemy or to run away to survive. (Sound familiar? Auditions can feel that way sometimes.)

Adrenaline is one of the chemicals that courses through your body under dangerous circumstances. It gives you an immediate burst of much-needed power and strength. Even if you're just feeling exhausted and uncertain of where you're going to find the energy to play your eighth show of the week, you can be certain that somewhere around thirty minutes before showtime, your body will begin to find the strength it needs, largely due to adrenaline and your own mental focus. All this use of adrenaline is extremely positive!

On the less positive side, the startle reflex can get overstimulated, and the outpouring of adrenaline isn't useful at all. It's not constructive to always be operating on nervous energy. This is like gunning a car's engine. It wears down the machine and tires it out. If you are constantly "on," this means you are always working at too high a pitch. It's tiring, exhausting, and can leave you emotionally and physically depleted.

There are times when the startle reflex is completely understandable. If a loud boom goes off outside your home, you may find yourself jumping. Theoretically, you react to the stimulus, process it, and return to your "normal state" as you release your reaction a moment or two later. But oftentimes this is not how it works.

Sometimes you react to the loud noise and hold on to the restrictive, almost crouching state for some time afterward. It's an emotional reaction to the unexpected noise. Sometimes there is anticipation of another noise. And for many of us, the startle reflex can happen often—dozens of times a day. That is something you can change. The first step is sensing the startle reflex and being aware of it.

Positive Change and Observation of the Self

A fundamental Buddhist belief is, "Change is inevitable, since everything is impermanent." Buddhists see change as natural. They sometimes use the analogy that life is like a river; a series of constantly changing moments, no two quite the same but joined together, which gives the impression of one continuous flowing movement. If one accepts this concept as true, why would anyone fight against change? Why are we dismayed by so many changes in our world?

I'm sympathetic to a dislike of change. Wanting things to stay the same seems to be a part of the human condition. But a lot of it has to do with fear. In an uncertain world, we're looking for something to hold on to. Everyone is familiar with fear; however, if you embrace change as inevitable and see it as a chance to expand rather than something to fight against, both life and art are easier.

Think of it this way: as a person and as an artist, you won't always be the same. In life and in art, you can be low-key when you want, or full steam ahead when that's called for. The main point is that it's your *choice*.

You can build awareness by observation, almost like a scientist. It's common for performers to observe strangers and think, "Where is that man going? Why is he in a hurry? I wonder why he wore that tie with that suit? Is he married? How many children does he have?" As an actor, you can apply the same skills to observing yourself.

When actors are at their best, they *don't judge people*. They don't judge the characters they are playing. When you are observing your self and expanding your awareness, *don't judge yourself*. Easy to say—but this takes practice. For some reason, almost all of us are quick to judge ourselves.

It's important to keep in mind that there is no need to push for results. We can discard the ideas of "standing up straight," "pushing your shoulders back," and "putting a book on top of your head." This will only lead to stiffening and forcing. We're looking to do the opposite: release, open up, and let go.

The Alexander Technique offers actors a *positive, constructive way of working*. An actor is often the object of extreme criticism. She is told that her voice is too high and metallic, her movement is stiff and awkward, her acting overly intellectualized, and her choices too obvious. However, I've noticed that if a teacher is supportive and sympathetic, encouraging and constructive, his or her student blossoms, new doors are opened, and bad habits tend to disappear.

This nonjudgmental, accepting approach allows actors to become aware of their bodies, their mental and physical tics, and make a conscious decision to stop and change. Some performers may feel that mind-body training is an unnecessary waste of time and money—"I just want to be myself, to be natural." But what may feel natural may actually be *habitual*. By "habitual" I mean something that is ingrained, or rigid. It is not a choice. Through good psycho-physical training, one can be freed of the habitual and revel in the truly natural.

Let's explore the first Alexander concept: *sense*. Through the senses, you will build and expand your awareness. This is the foundation of all the work we're doing together. The more you use your senses effectively, the more centered and grounded your acting work will become. The more discriminating and reliable your senses become, the more they feed your acting.

Observing Yourself in a Mirror

This can be one of the most difficult exercises for people to do. The tendency to want to "fix" things you don't like in yourself is almost irresistible. Stanislavski, in his autobiography, *My Life In Art*, describes spending most of one summer working with self-observation in a mirror. Some might tell you to adjust what you see as the "problems" in your body, I am suggesting you take note and don't try to "fix it" for now. Remind yourself that you're *increasing your awareness*; that's all you need focus on at the moment.

- Stand in front of a full-length mirror.
- Close your eyes and bring yourself into your habitual stance, the one that feels "normal" to you.
- Open your eyes.
- Observe yourself, as if you were looking at someone else. Try not to judge, but simply gather information.
- Take a look at yourself from head to toe: Is your head balanced at the end of your spine? Is your neck easily elongated? Is one shoulder higher than the other? Is your torso straight, or does it pull to one side? Are your hips relatively even? Does your lower back arch or collapse down? What's going on with your legs and arms?
- Notice your breathing: Do you hold your breath, or make it shallow? Do you breathe more into one side of your ribcage than the other? Is your breath even or uneven? How does your breathing affect your stance?
- Don't "fix" anything—just look at yourself as you would look at someone else.

Observing Yourself in Movement

This is an exercise I developed at the Actors Studio MFA Program. I shot video footage of everyone at the beginning of each semester. At the end of the three-year program, I showed the students the videos so they could see how their stance and movement had changed over six semesters. They were often shocked at how they looked in the beginning. When you watch the video you make of yourself, I would caution you to go easy on yourself. It's not about getting down on yourself. It's a way that you can learn more about how you use yourself. After watching the video, make a date with a friend in three months, and take another video. If you work on yourself for just a few minutes a day with exercises from this book, you will see positive changes over the course of time.

- Observe yourself in a large mirror. Even better, ask a friend to film you with a handheld device.
- Move as you would in everyday life, when you're not thinking about it.
- Walk back and forth across the room several times.
- Stand up and sit down a number of times.
- Reach up, as if you are getting something from a high shelf.

- Go up onto your toes a few times, as you do habitually.
- Bend down to pick something up off the floor.
- Switch roles. Now you video your friend. You'll learn from watching what she does.

Looking at Old Photos or Videos of Yourself

When you look at photographs from other times in your life, you can be more objective about what you see. Analyze how you are using your body: standing, sitting, walking. Observe your body language in candid photos of you speaking with other people. How close do you sit or stand to the other person? Do you tend to lean into or away from the other person? How comfortable do you look? Compare old photos and videos with current photographs. Note how your body is similar to and different from years ago. Focus on gathering information rather than the things you'd like to "fix."

- Gather photos of yourself from when you were a child, a teenager, and/ or a young adult. If you have old videos, even better.
- Look at yourself without paying much attention to clothing and hairstyles. Give your attention to your body.
- Notice yourself from head to toe. Do you see physical habits similar to your current ones? Certain ways of standing or holding yourself? Do you put most of your weight on one foot? Are there twists in your body? Does your head pull to one side?
- Do you notice if habits increase or decrease over time?
- If you have family photographs, do you notice any family traits? Do your siblings or parents use their bodies in a similar way?
- Photos in bathing suits or shorts and T-shirts can be revealing. If you have any of these photos, can you see things about yourself that aren't obvious when you're wearing other kinds of clothing?

The World's Simplest Sense Memory

Some people find sense memory exercises challenging. To keep things easy, let's create a *new* sense memory. This exercise focuses on the sensation of hot or cold and is useful if you ever have to pick up a stone-cold coffee cup, for example, and pretend it's hot. It can also be applied in many other acting situations, even those that have nothing to do with temperature.

What's it like to be rudely awakened in the middle of the night? What do you feel in your body when you're startled awake? What do you feel in your body when someone screams at you? Do you shrink and hunch your shoulders in a defensive posture? Or do you feel angry and puff yourself up? If you can't remember how you react in your body in such situations, you can pay attention to your reactions the next time something like that happens to you.

Another time that sensory work can be of practical help is when you're acting in a film and the actual weather is different from the weather in the screenplay. For instance, you can use sense memory if you have to indicate through your body language that it's a hot day when in actuality it's freezing and you're only in a T-shirt.

- Get a hot cup of coffee or tea. Or pull something out of the freezer that's cold: a bag of peas or a tub of ice cream.
- If necessary, to keep from burning your hands on the hot or cold items, you can use a tissue to cover the object.
- Put the tissue on the object and take hold of it with your hands.
- Feel the shape: round, curved, square, or uneven.
- Feel the heat or the cold coming from the object.
- How do you feel about the shape and the heat or cold? Is it pleasant or does it bother you? Do you feel compelled to have the drink? Are you tempted to eat the ice cream?
- Does it remind you of another time when you held a similar object?
- Are you able to hold the object for some time comfortably, or do you become restless?
- How do you feel as you continue to hold the object? Is the tea cooling off? Is this ice cream beginning to melt?
- What is happening with the rest of your body as you hold onto the object? Are you relatively comfortable and upright, or are you slumped over to hold it? Are you able to focus on the object and your body at the same time, or do you have to do it sequentially?
- What happens to your breathing?
- What do you feel emotionally?

Releasing with Your Eyes Open

Many people say that they can't relax with their eyes open—that closing their eyes allows them to focus on themselves and let go. The problem is, most of the time when you're acting, your eyes are open.

Among other things, this exercise helps you avoid "fixing" your gaze. "Glazed" eyes often are associated with overconcentration. Anytime your eyes stiffen, the rest of your body stiffens as well. The eyes become tense as you try hard at something. Giving up the idea of concentrating hard helps you achieve an easier, more released focus. When your eyes are released, your whole body releases.

- Sit comfortably in a chair or lie down on the floor with a book under your head and your knees bent.
- Sense your own breathing.
- Allow your whole body to ease into a more released state.
- Close your eyes.
- Sense yourself, starting at the top of your head, and move all the way through down to your feet. Stay with that for a few minutes.
- Allow yourself to sigh a few times.
- Keep your breathing easy.
- Allow your whole face to let go.
- Slowly open your eyes for a few moments. Then close them again.
- Remind yourself to breathe easily.
- Sense the freedom in your body.
- Slowly open your eyes again and leave them open.
- Continue to stay easy in your body, and your breathing.
- Remind yourself that you can be released with your eyes open.

Dead Weight

This exercise allows you to experience the difference between "live" and "dead" weight. You can feel this when you hold a child or a pet. There is one perceived weight when they are awake and supporting their own weight. There is another when the child or pet is asleep: it's heavier, "dead." It's the same thing in your own body. When you are balanced and coordinated, your movement will seem lighter, more graceful, even "floaty" at times. If you are tight and slumped downward, you will feel heavier; it's harder to move. This is a simple yet striking example of how what you are thinking, and what your intention is, becomes manifest in your body.

- Sit in a straight-backed chair. Have both your feet on the floor, your hands in your lap.
- Take a few moments to compose yourself. Be aware of your body in the chair. Sense your breathing. Aware of yourself in the space.

- Consciously make yourself very heavy. Your intention is that you are dead weight. Energyless.
- Now imagine that you weigh one thousand pounds. You are very, very heavy. Almost immobile.
- With that intention in mind, stand up out of the chair. Note what that feels like.
- You still weigh one thousand pounds. Sit down in the chair. How does the movement feel when your body comes into the chair?
- Return to "neutral sitting." You no longer weigh one thousand pounds. Your hands are back in your lap. Be aware of your easy breathing. Allow the first part of the exercise to fade away.
- Have your intention be that your body is hollow. It's very light and easy.
- Now imagine that your body is full of helium. The helium helps your body float up to its fullest height.
- Stand up out of the chair. Note what that feels like.
- Stand easily at your full height: you are "live weight." Light and free.
- Sensing your own lightness, glide down into the chair. What does that feel like?
- Sit in the chair, aware of your own repose.

Postural Extremes

This is the easiest way I've found to let your body know what you *don't* want it to do, a way of exploring your body's extremes. Slump down aggressively, exaggerating the motion and getting a sense of what it feels like to be there for a period of time. Then adopt a military posture. Hold on to it. It often feels stilted after only a few moments. What you're looking for is something in between these two extremes.

- Sit comfortably in a straight-backed chair in a "neutral" position.
- Give your attention to your breathing. Allow it to be as free as possible.
- Intentionally slump into your worst slump. Imagine you've been slumped for hours watching television or hunched over the computer. Let your body be tight and pulled in.
- Make a mental note of what you feel in your body. Initially, it may feel relatively comfortable to you. But after a while you may come to feel less comfortable.

- Allow that feeling to go. Take an easy breath and return to your neutral sitting.
- Then take on "military posture." Pull yourself up from your middle, stiffen your spine into a straight line, pull your shoulders back, and lock your head into a fixed position.
- Stay this way for some time. How does this feel?
- Return to neutral sitting.
- Breathe easily; let out a few easy sighs.
- Find a middle ground between those two extremes. Sit easily, at your full height, without strain or force.
- Know that this is what you're looking for. An easy balance.

Your Body as a Totality

By making lists and drawing yourself, you can approach your acting instrument from a different angle. It can help you discover valuable information about yourself and help you realize, in a visceral way, that you are a unified whole.

- Get a piece of paper and a pen, your laptop, or your handheld device.
- Write down the parts of your body you feel good about and why. Perhaps you like the way they look, or they feel good, or they seem to function well.
- List the parts of your body you don't feel good about and why.
- Make a list of the parts of your body that rarely enter your consciousness. For instance, many people don't think about the sides of their body, their ankles, their wrists, or the backs of their heads.
- Which parts of your body hurt or ache? Is anything numb?
- Draw a picture of your body as you experience it. Do this intuitively, without thinking much about it.
- After you're finished, study what you've drawn.
- Do you experience your body as a totality or as a series of discrete parts? Write about that. How do your movement and posture reflect your experience of your own body?
- How do you experience the mind-body connection, both in everyday life and in your acting work?

Your Body Experience

When you allow yourself to write at length without thinking much about it and without censoring yourself, quite a bit can come to light. Some of your own beliefs might surprise you. You can also do this exercise with a trusted friend and see how your perceptions and those of others might differ.

- Complete the following sentences:
- My body ...
- My posture ...
- My movement ...
- My breathing ...
- My voice ...
- My acting ...
- When people look at me ...
- Write a few paragraphs about how you felt about your body as a child.
- Write about what you'd like your body to ideally be like when you are in your seventies or eighties.
- Write about how you feel about your mind-body, right now, at this moment.

3

Poise, Flow, and Choice

You might be surprised when I tell you that I don't want you to improve your *posture*. Most people think they understand what that word means. It conjures up out-of-date images of walking with a book on your head, military style, or of pulling your shoulders back, sucking in your "gut," and keeping your back rigidly straight.

While there is nothing wrong with the word "posture" per se, there is a problem with people's conception of what it is. Most people perceive posture as something layered on, maintained with exertion, something static. They often express the wish to "hold on to it" or "freeze it in place." Is this comfortable, or even possible? You may need to discard the idea of being someone with "perfect posture." A highly trained, balanced, and poised body will do just fine.

When it comes to your body and movement, the objective is to be *natural*. You had organically good balance and movement when you were a child. If you watch most young children up to the age of about six, they are graceful, coordinated, and elongated. The child is interested in the world around her; her movement comes out of her motivations—to reach for a new toy, to walk across the room to fall into her mother's arms, to pet the dog sitting next to her. She is not trying to have "good posture," but she does have a wonderful, natural use of herself. Her movements are in the moment, unforced and unimpaired. It's rare to see this in a grown adult, but it's certainly possible. And that's what we're going for.

To help "unclog" the natural flow within you, consider the Alexander concept of *use affects functioning*. That means if your body is balanced, your *movement* and *functioning* will be balanced. Conversely, if you tighten your neck muscles, your head pulls back and down onto your neck. Your head weighs between eight and ten pounds; this puts that amount of weight down not only onto the neck itself but also onto your shoulders, torso, and even your arms and legs. It puts a downward drag on your whole body. It's like driving down the highway with the emergency brake on.

If you stop compressing your head onto your neck, your head will balance, and your whole body naturally lengthens. When you maintain this coordination as you are moving, with your head leading the movement and your body following, it helps to coordinate everything: your body, your movement, and your functioning.

You can see this head-leading-and-body-following coordination (what Alexander called *primary control*) when a horse walks: the head leads, the torso succeeds it harmoniously. It's the same for a dog or a cat—and for humans. When you release up to your fullest height, up toward the ceiling, it helps all motion become more gliding and smooth as you move forward through space. It's important to remember: *there is no one correct "position"* for your head on top of the spine. It's *balance* that you want to maintain in activity and movement.

Famous people who have displayed this wonderful use of the body and excellent use of primary control include the dancers Fred Astaire and Margot Fonteyn, the boxer Muhammad Ali, the pianist Arthur Rubinstein, and the soccer player Pelé. Beautiful, flowing movement was part of their artistic and athletic expression. Through the superlative use of their bodies, they are able to express the inexpressible.

Poise Opens the Door to Profound Personal Change

Poise gives you the freedom to achieve profound change. You cannot change if you keep doing the same thing over and over again. In order to circumvent your habits, Alexander suggested you give yourself a split second to pause to allow yourself to choose your own behavior—to choose what you want to do next.

This is a radical idea. Everyone is pressed for time. Even taking a split second for yourself seems an impossible luxury. People feel they must keep moving forward, with ever-increasing momentum. When so many things are coming at you from so many angles, it's hard to think straight, then this is a good moment to pause. In fact, this is an imperative moment to pause.

There is a wonderful expression from the 1930s: *Pause for poise*. I wish it would come back into fashion. I understand the necessity for multitasking and twenty-four-hour connectivity, but we are human beings with limits. Pausing helps. Pauses are microbreaks. It's a challenge, but train yourself to take them. You can pause anytime, anywhere. And pauses can last for only a split second.

Alexander called this pausing *inhibition*—meaning stopping old, unconstructive habits—not to be confused with the Freudian notion of inhibition, which is about repressing emotions. I have dubbed the Alexander kind of inhibition "poise," partly because it is an active rather than a passive word. It is a kind of balancing or suspension, like what a trapeze artist does when she moves delicately across the high wire, constantly making micromovements to maintain her equilibrium. Like the trapeze artist, we can be suspended when we choose to be. Another metaphor for suspension is a child's swing. There is a moment when the swing goes all the way up and you are suspended in the air before you swing in the other direction. It's a wonderful moment, when you seem to float in midair. That's what poise can feel like.

For example, if you have a habit of tensing your neck and tightening your shoulders as you sing, the crux of the tightening probably happens right before you sing, at the moment that is called the *onset*. That's the moment you take in the air, right before you open your mouth to burst into song. Unfortunately, that is also the moment when your mental worries ("Am I really going to be able to hit that high note?"), your emotional worries ("This director has never liked me"), and your physical habits (tight neck, stiff tongue) converge. That's when the mental and emotional concerns can amplify the physical habits and the moment when poise can be most useful.

Far from being restrictive, pausing for poise is freeing. This relates to the Zen concept of *beginner's mind*, a cultivated attitude of an open mind with few preconceptions. The author Shunryu Suzuki wrote in his book *Zen Mind, Beginner's Mind*, "In the beginner's mind there are many possibilities, in the expert's mind there are few." It is especially useful for an expert in a field to continue to practice beginner's mind, not expecting she knows all the answers, even with her expertise. This practice also tends to keep people much more physically and mentally released.

Poise is a pragmatic way to "be here now." It brings you to the practical place of "Here is a step I can take to bring about a change—right here, right now." Practicing these valuable "moments of suspension" each day shows that you have a belief and investment in the future. Rather than doing things "the same old way every same old day," you will have a sense of being in charge of your own destiny.

Personal Experiences of Poise

When I was a child I learned swimming with a swimming coach. She was gently encouraging and helped me build my confidence. The backstroke turned out to be my strongest stroke, and she invited me to take part in a swim meet. It was an exciting prospect, but also a little scary.

Suddenly it was the day of the meet. It was a large indoor pool. There were bleachers set up on either side of the pool filled with parents, families, and other people: it was a packed house. While waiting my turn, I had some butterflies, and wondered how I would do; I'd never been at a swim meet before. Finally, my turn came. I looked down the row of other swimmers. My coach didn't tell me that this was an open-age category! I was eight and small for my age. There were other boys who looked thirteen and were much taller and bigger than I was. I panicked. I thought, "There is no way I'm going to win this match."

Of course, I didn't know what the Alexander Technique was at that time, and I didn't know what inhibition or suspension to attain poise was. But I instinctively used a version of it. I tried to calm myself through thinking, "Forget about the other guys. Focus on yourself." I was holding on to the side of the pool. I thought to myself, "Choose a point on the wall behind the starting gate. Focus on that point. Don't think about anything else, and move away from that point as fast as you can." This happened in a matter of seconds. Suddenly the race began; I pushed away from the wall as hard as I could. I could hear the screams of the spectators dimly, and sensed the splashing of the water all around me from the other swimmers, but somehow I was able to follow my own instructions and stay focused on moving away from the point on the wall as fast as I could. I paid attention to the process as opposed to the results. It was over in a flash, and I won.

Suspension has helped me professionally as an actor in many ways. It can help you turn on a dime in rehearsal. Once I played the character of Claudio in *Measure for Measure*. Claudio is sentenced to death for impregnating an unmarried woman. In one scene, he begs his sister to help him by interceding on his behalf with the man who is in charge, Angelo. His sister, Isabella, is a virtuous young woman, a novice nun, but Angelo is interested in her sexually. Claudio is fighting for his life, and begs his sister to use whatever means necessary to save him. In the scene, I used all kinds of tactics to try and convince my sister: rational argument, emotional pleas, and appealing to her sisterly devotion. Then one time in rehearsal a thought crossed my mind: "What else can I do to convince her?" I let myself not know for a split second (poise) and then I kissed her on the lips, which surprised the actor and reminded her of what Angelo wanted to do as well. My usual behavior might have been to have the idea but then think, "No, that's going too far." But I allowed myself the freedom to go someplace unexpected, and it turned out to be one of the most effective moments in the scene.

"Saying no" to a habit is a "positive no." It is "saying yes" to new experiences. Train yourself to take your time and to learn *when* to pause. Take small minibreaks throughout the day. They can last anywhere from a few seconds to thirty minutes during a session of constructive rest on the floor.

This pause is a deliberate suspending of time and a gift to yourself that allows you to experience something new.

Awareness, Poise, and Flow

One of the most important aspects of the Alexander Technique is what Alexander termed *directions*—a concept I've dubbed *flow*. Building on the two previous steps leading to it, awareness and poise, flow gives you practical, self-guided steps to help you change your tension habits. Rather than punitive self-talk ("Why can't you stand up straight?" "Just look at yourself. You look awful!"), the Alexander Technique suggests conscious, gentle reminders. They are as follows:

- *Let my neck be free …*

The first and most important word in this phrase is "let." Don't try to force your neck to be free. Just think it. If you asked yourself to tense up, you could do that. Here you are training yourself to do the opposite. Rather than doing something to *make* your neck free, you *allow* the muscles of your neck to soften, release, and let go. It's a quiet thought that originates in your brain, travels through your nervous system, and ends up with the muscles that respond to your thought.

Often, when your neck is tight, your head retracts back and down on the top of the spine. So the next phrase is:

- *To let my head go forward and up …*

"Forward" does not mean you have put your head in front of you in space. It means letting go of the tension that is retracting your head back, so that your head naturally rotates a tiny bit forward. It's like dropping your nose a quarter of an inch. If your head pushes down on your spine, it sets up a series of compensating tensions throughout your whole body. When you release your head slightly forward and up, it relieves the compression, and your spine releases in an upward direction, toward the ceiling. Your head will always be releasing away from the top of your spine, whatever position you are in.

The next suggestion is:

- *To let my torso lengthen and widen …*

This phrase also begins with the words "to let," reminding you that you are using thought rather than muscular effort. You release the downward pressure on your torso, which allows it to naturally lengthen without your having to force it. Your spine lets go into its optimal balanced length, so you are not ramrod straight, nor are you slumped over in a shortened stature. When you widen, you allow your muscles to release out to the sides, away from the central axis of your spine. As we've discussed, slumping or military posture are the two extremes you'd like to avoid. Lengthening and widening work together to let you expand to your fullest dimensions. When it happens, you can "take your space" in the room, which gives you a naturally increased stage presence and charisma. You look like a person to be taken seriously.

Onto the next thought:

- *To let my legs and arms release away from my torso…*

Your torso (including your pelvis) releases up, in the direction of your head. At the same time, your legs release in the opposite direction, away from your hip joints. It's almost like you're a piece of elastic that is gently being stretched in two directions. When you are standing, the leg muscles will lengthen toward the floor when you remind yourself not to stiffen and pull them up into the hip joints. The knees are neither bent nor locked back. They are straight without being rigid. Imagine your torso balancing easily on top of your legs. Sometimes your arms may contract up into your underarms. This can result in the shoulders slightly raising and rounding forward. Think about allowing your arms to give over to gravity and hang easily at your sides.

Then:

- *Let my shoulders widen.*

When the tension in your shoulders releases, your shoulders and chest tend to widen out to both sides. This helps to free up and deepen your breathing. There is an expansiveness and openness. This takes you out of what could be interpreted as either a defensive or aggressive stance. Rather, it's an open, accessible, "neutral" stance, a way of being that naturally attracts a positive kind of attention. You look like somebody other people want to know.

I've broken this italicized sentence into parts to explain it more fully. But when you say these thoughts to yourself, remember that all the phrases form one sentence: *Let my neck be free, to let my head go forward and up, to let my torso lengthen and widen, to let my legs and arms release away from my torso, and let my shoulders widen.* In this sentence, you're dealing with your whole self—your totality. It's easy to fall into thinking about parts, especially if they are painful or uncomfortable, but I'm sure as you practice you will find it easier to keep your whole self in mind.

It's important to recognize, too, that you can't *impel* your spine to lengthen. To achieve freer usage, you (1) become aware of yourself and what you're doing, (2) pause to allow yourself to come out of your familiar physical habits, and (3) remind yourself of the process instructions that are connected to flow. You keep this process going as you start moving or as you act in a scene or monologue. The process instructions help liberate you from your habits, leaving yourself at your most open for your acting.

As you become more familiar with these subtle suggestions, they will have deeper meaning for you as you see them affecting you. You want your muscles to be released—to do only as much work as they need to do for the activities at hand. Anything extra is excessive tension. This goes for something as simple as raising your arm or as complex as speaking the verse in *Hamlet*. When your muscles are released and working as a unified whole, you're being efficient. Then you can give the performance you imagined.

As you work through this process, you'll also find it helpful to slowly change your mental concepts. You probably don't like your tension, restriction, or pain—but you may be used to it. You may have the idea that being tightly bound, rigid in your muscles, and compressed down on yourself is "just how I am." It may not feel possible to change. But the manner in which you think of the flow suggestions is different from other ways of thinking. It's not in any way forced or pushed. You can imagine talking to yourself in the kind, low tone you would use to speak to a close friend or small child. You deserve to be spoken to gently and patiently.

Flow will help you with many things: stage fright (performance anxiety), self-consciousness, awkward movement, poor body stance, restricted breathing and vocal production, and the relationship you have with your fellow actors and the audience.

One of the best things you can do for yourself is "remembering to remember"—remembering to work on yourself for a few minutes in the morning and again in the evening. Throughout the rest of the day you can do what I call "dropping in": as you are in the midst of doing something, ask yourself, "How am I sitting? How am I walking? How am I performing this speech?" That's using awareness. Then you can take a few moments to go through the poise-flow process. The more you do that throughout the day, the more you begin to incorporate this process into your life, so it will be there when you need it.

Empire State Building

If you visit the Empire State Building in New York and travel to the top, try this exercise. You can try it in other very tall buildings as well. Close your eyes and feel the slight swaying of the building. It is so tall, it's built to move in the wind. If it wasn't, it would crack. We need to balance and very slightly move as we are balancing as well. The only way that you will be stock-still is if you stiffen. You may need to appear to be still in scenes in a film or a play. The micromovements I'm talking about will not be visible to the audience. Try thinking about this when waiting in line or looking at paintings in a museum. You'll find that "active standing" is less tiring and less stressful on your back. Standing is not a "position" but a poising—a constantly and subtly changing equilibrium.

- Stand with your feet slightly apart.
- Think of your Alexander "flow" reminders (*Let my neck be free, to let my head go forward and up, to let my torso lengthen and widen, to let my legs and arms release away from my torso, and let my shoulders widen*) and of gently lengthening in an upward direction.
- Rather than "standing still," think of balancing.
- You may sense yourself slightly swaying, moving around on your feet slightly. Allow the micromovements to happen without forcing them to happen.
- Close your eyes.
- Sense the slight movements forward, back, and to the sides as you balance. Try not to stiffen your legs or lock your knees.
- Keep breathing. If you tune in to it, you may become aware of your breathing stimulating the slight swayings.
- Allow your eyes to open.
- Sense if you can stay aware of your own balancing and also be aware of the environment.

Making Mistakes on Purpose

So many of us are afraid of making a mistake. This fear is heightened when you are in front of people—in class, rehearsals, or performance. What if you forget a word? Make a mistake in your blocking? Make a poor acting choice? These things can feel like life-and-death issues—I know, I've felt them myself. But from my vantage point now, I would say, "It's not the end of the world." In fact, it can feel tremendously freeing to act out the "worst-case scenario" and purposely make "mistakes." Then you see firsthand that it's not so terrible. Often this exercise makes people laugh. The further you take it, the more ridiculous it is (in a good way).

- Read a speech out loud from a play or novel. Read as you would normally.
- Read the speech again. Make mistakes on purpose. Mispronounce words. Mix up the order of the words. Make poor acting choices.
- Exaggerate your mistakes. Make them ridiculously obvious.

- Do the speech with absurd and inappropriate gestures.
- Whatever the meaning of the speech, indicate the opposite as you are reading.
- See if you can read part of the speech backward. Start with the last word and read backward.
- Translate the speech into gibberish and speak nonsense words.
- Now read the speech simply and as truthfully as you can.

Critical Moment

This exercise is one of the best ways to practice poise. The critical moment right before you speak, sing, dance, or move is a heightened one, and often your habits will reappear in a heightened form; they become much more evident. It can feel like you have no power to change. The good news is that in these moments it's easier to become aware of your habits and identify what you want to work on. Take my word: you can change; the answer lies in taking small steps.

- Choose a speech or song that you like but find a little difficult.
- Stand in front of a large mirror.
- See if you can observe yourself nonjudgmentally. Don't do anything different from what you would do when you're not looking in a mirror.
- Speak or sing the beginning of the speech or song.
- What do you see in your body as you begin—especially at the onset, the very beginning? If you're not sure, do it several times.
- You may notice a slight tensing of your neck or a forward displacement of your neck when you begin. You may also notice a retraction of your head back and down. Perhaps your shoulders tighten up or round forward.
- See what happens if you think to allow your *neck to be free, your head to release forward and up, and your torso to lengthen and widen.* Stay with that thought as you prepare to speak or sing, but at the last moment do something else. Raise your arm or take a step instead. You're circumventing your habit before it happens.
- Think through your Alexander thoughts, as above, and allow yourself to ease into the speech or song. How is this different from the first time you did it?

"Have You Thought About How Difficult This Is?"

Maybe this has already happened to you in real life—you've gotten lectures from well-meaning people who are trying to protect you from a life in the arts, maybe even to "save you from yourself." It's challenging not to tense up when people go into these monologues, especially if the person talking is adamant about the topic. It's a good exercise to listen with one charitable ear while you focus on keeping your breathing even and deep and leaving your body as free as possible. Don't get defensive or emotional. Just listen and "stay with yourself."

- You'll need a friend for this exercise.
- Find a quiet space.
- Face each other, either standing or sitting. Be fairly close together.
- Have your friend give you what I call the "Have you thought about how difficult this is?" lecture. Your friend can go to town, listing all the reasons why acting is a bad idea as a profession—the uneven flow of income, lack of guaranteed work, the odds are against you, and so on.
- See if you can remain calm as your friend lectures you. The Alexander directions may help. Make sure you keep your breathing easy.
- Switch roles and lecture your friend. Your friend tries to remain calm.

Counting

Sometimes people are a bit confused by the idea of suspending or pausing. They are afraid to move, so they freeze in place. This is the opposite of what is meant by poise. Suspension is just a moment when you give yourself time and space to consider what you want to do next.

- Count to ten out loud.
- Notice what happens in your body as you speak.
- Count to ten a few more times.
- Do you notice any points of tension? The back of your neck? The front of your throat, near your larynx? Your shoulders or lower back?
- Pause for a moment. Don't freeze; just pause briefly.
- Ask yourself to be easy in your body and your breath.

- "Suspend" your tension habits. Say a "positive no" to them and "yes" to a new kind of behavior: freedom in your throat, shoulders, and back.
- Think your Alexander thoughts: *neck free, head forward and up, torso lengthening and widening.*
- Count to ten, thinking of your neck being easy and your back long.
- Pause for a moment to let yourself return to an easy neutral.
- Count to ten more loudly. Ask yourself not to tighten just because you're speaking more loudly.
- Pause for a moment and allow yourself to breathe easily.
- Count to twenty-five (breathing whenever necessary), pausing slightly on the words "five," "ten," "fifteen," and "twenty." During the brief pause, remind yourself to stay easy in your body and keep your breath easy.

Up Energy Through Your Whole Body

This is a fundamental exercise for helping to get the Alexander principles going in your body. It helps to bring you back to your natural, easy state, where you're meant to be organically. It's an ideal place from which to act.

- Stand with your feet comfortably apart.
- *Think your neck free, head forward and up, and torso lengthening and widening. Arms hanging freely at your sides. Legs releasing away from your torso.*
- Gently think up through your torso, up along your spine, deep inside your body.
- Allow your arms to float all the way out from your sides, parallel to the floor.
- Think length through your torso, width across your chest and shoulders, and let your arms gently stretch out to each side. Let your legs gently lengthen toward the floor.
- Let your arms float back down to your sides.
- Let them float back out to the sides, then back down to your sides.
- Allow your arms to stretch easily all the way up toward the ceiling. Be aware of a soft lengthening up the front, back, and sides of your body.
- Float your arms back down toward your sides, but stay with the thought of "up" through your torso as your arms come down.
- Repeat a second time. Let your arms come up toward the ceiling, then come up onto your toes. Thinking of reaching up into infinity.
- Then come back to center. Remember the gentle upward lengthening continuing through your body, even when standing still.

Anti-Berating

Sometimes the stressors in your life come from the outside, and sometimes they come from the inside in the form of negative self-talk. I see the results in actors and their work all the time. They get in their own way. You've internalized certain (often erroneous) beliefs about yourself, and your mind-body reacts to them. These insecurities can spring up at any time, especially in important moments like auditions, callbacks, and important performances. But if you start to chip away at some of these belief systems, it can help you deal with these moments more easily. Examining these ideas about yourself is like taking old clothes from the bottom of your closet. Give them a little air and a good long look, and maybe you can throw them away.

- Take out your mind-body journal.
- Make a list of the ways you berate yourself—about the use of your body, your movement, your mental-physical ways of doing things.
- Make another list of the parts of your body that you are less than fond of.
- List the things about your own acting that you are less than happy about.
- Sketch out a list of self-criticisms that originated with things other people said about you.
- Look at your lists. Is your body that much worse than everyone else's? Would you be this hard on a close friend?
- Look at the list of things you might want to change in your own acting. Are your acting issues really that much more challenging than everyone else's?
- List the ways you might be a bit easier on yourself in your mind-body issues, and in your acting issues.
- Consider the idea that maybe the issues are not quite as entrenched as you thought.

Practicing Flow

This is one of the most elemental exercises and can be practiced every day. You don't necessarily need to put special time aside to work on these self-guiding thoughts. You can think them as you go about your daily activities: getting ready in the morning, while you are eating, reading, or watching a movie. These directions originate in your mind, travel through your nervous system, and bring your thought to your muscles. Gradually, you will embody your thoughts are guiding you to be. It can be your own personal Manifest Destiny—to expand yourself to your fullest potential.

- Sit comfortably in a chair that has support, or lie down on the floor, a paperback book under your head, with your knees bent.
- Have a sense of where you are. Your body on the chair, or against the floor.
- Sense your breath flowing in and out of you. Remember that there is always a gentle motion. Nothing is static in the body.
- Think through your flow thoughts: *Let your neck be free, to let your head go forward and up, to let your torso lengthen and widen, to let your arms and legs release away from your body.*
- Remember that you are mind-body. That your thought can profoundly affect your physicality.
- Be here now. In the present moment. The past and the future will be there when you're ready to think about them.
- Rethink your flow thoughts gently for a few minutes. Flow is a renewal; it's not a position.

4

The Use of Your Self

In the last two chapters we dealt with how to sense things in your mind and body—your self—and how to begin to constructively change things you want to alter. Your sensory awareness helps you prepare the ground for the two other components in the Alexander process—poise and flow. As you practice these three concepts, they blend together organically and help you with what Alexander called "the use of the self." This means *how* you are using your mind-body: in everyday movement and functioning, which is important in your daily life, but also in acting, where it is essential.

As you practice, you'll find you're more able to mold yourself and the quality of your movement in order to bring to life the various characters you play. A skillful actor uses body language as a fluent and expressive subverbal communication; the manner in which you move reveals something about the inner life of your character that's not possible to communicate in words. *Your body language will expose the human behavior* that lives deep within your character: a vital part of the storytelling.

For example, let's consider the act of lying. Leaving aside a character's motivation for lying, sometimes an actor makes it a bit too obvious to the audience. Maybe she is concerned the audience won't understand she is lying. But in real life, lying is often hard to detect. People often lie quite well, and most of the time they don't want to be found out. Nevertheless, studies show that when people prevaricate, their bodies sometimes betray the lie, even if they express the lie with conviction. These signs are subtle. Sometimes their eyes will dart to the side just at the moment of the lie. Or they do something physically awkward, like clanking a spoon against a coffee mug. It can be the tone or manner in which they are speaking or an emotional reaction that seems to come out of nowhere. The audience will understand this type of subtle behavior within the context of the scene.

Another example is dramatic irony: the character says one thing when she really believes another. She's not lying—she is trying to make herself believe what she's saying. Again, this action can be shown effectively through a subtle use of the voice or body. The deeper meaning is in the subtext, which you can transmit in a nuanced way. The use of the self is an invaluable tool in your acting arsenal, and you'll be able to use it to great effect onstage and also in film, where human behavior can be especially detailed and subtle when viewed in a close-up.

The use of your self is not only what's happening in your body but also how you "use" yourself mentally and emotionally. There's no way to separate the three components; they are a triumvirate. For example, one way I've misused myself is my old habit of driving myself too hard. This had physical manifestations: I used to hunch over my homework, my shoulders pulled up and my neck pulled down toward the desk. What drove this physical behavior was my mental attitude of "I've got to work very hard, get good grades, and get ahead." My primal drive was my idea "I have to be a good actor. I've got to bear down." This was an essential part of my use that I was very invested in. Sound familiar?

Even if you don't completely share my old habit of overworking, there are other ways of pushing yourself. Some people say, "It's all good," trying to make themselves believe it when they don't, deep down. Even people who may seem devil-may-care on the surface may want something badly while hiding this from the world and maybe even from themselves.

The Use of Your Self Affects Your Functioning

We can't separate our emotions from the general use of ourselves in life or in our acting work. In my case, worrying about doing well, wanting to please my teachers, and showing them how well I could do was both an emotional and a mental drive for me. I was quick, organized, hardworking, disciplined, and creative, but also physically and mentally tight, too quick to doubt myself, and uncertain of my abilities. This phenomenon is what Alexander called *use affects functioning*; how I used my mind-body affected my own functioning.

Even if your issues manifest differently, the "use affects functioning" paradigm will come into play. For instance, some actors find it challenging to get motivated, to get themselves out there into the performing arts world. For some reason, they can't bring themselves to find out about the auditions coming up, or if they get a callback, maybe they can't bring themselves to get there. They may have ideas about doing their own productions, but find it too difficult to put all the details together or find a team of colleagues to work with. Sometimes people might be fearful of what could happen, what the outcome might be, or might be confused over where to start. Getting more balanced in yourself will help you get clearer about what's right for you. This clarity and sense of equilibrium within yourself can be imperative in building a personally satisfying career in the arts.

Let's examine what you do on the evening before an important audition. Do you stay up half the night, overeating and drinking, wake up late the next day, throw on whatever clothes are at hand, and dash to the audition just in time, or even late? Or do you try to get plenty of sleep the night before, spend the time before the audition reviewing the script, working on your character's intentions, do a short physical and vocal warm-up, and get to the audition in plenty of time? Okay, I've stacked the deck here and given a fairly black-and-white example to make my point—but there are many gradations between these two extremes.

Another example of how improved use leads to improved functioning is the practice of setting aside a few minutes every day to do mental-physical-vocal workouts: fifteen minutes is excellent. Ten minutes is fine if that's the time you've got. Perhaps you'll be able to squeeze in a ten-minute workout in the morning and five or ten minutes in the evening. It is so easy to say, "I have no time to do that," but we can all find ten minutes to work on ourselves and pockets of twenty minutes at a time to work with colleagues once a week or every two weeks. These pockets of work time are invaluable to your craft and to the business side of your professional life. A fundamental element in this is training yourself to spend those ten minutes well: with calm focus, perseverance, and patience.

Natural Performances

Sometimes members of the general public may unfairly criticize certain actors as being "always the same." These actors choose to work within a relatively narrow palette. They may embody a certain kind of character a number of times. But this does not mean that they are lazy, unskilled, or are "just being themselves," the inference being that it's quite easy to be yourself in front of the camera or a live audience. Nothing could be further from the truth.

I invite any audience member to try to see what it's like. What happens when you put someone who is not used to performing in front of a camera or on a stage? Sweat beads form on her forehead, her eyes dart or go blank, and her voice quavers. Suddenly, intelligent people can't remember the simplest facts. That's because acting is a skill that takes a lot of talent and training to do with excellence. Usually when someone says an actor is just "being herself" this betrays a lack of understanding of what the art of acting is.

The list of skilled naturalistic actors who appear to be doing "nothing" on camera is a long one. They may seem to be "doing nothing" because they are so skilled. You don't notice them acting; they are living their roles. In addition, many of these performers whom audiences criticize often struggle to win parts that would show a wider range of what they could do. Then the same audiences do not want to see them in other kinds of roles.

There are also some actors who are noted for the versatility, most famously Meryl Streep, Johnny Depp, and Daniel Day-Lewis. These are actors who use a broad palette when playing their roles. They are adept at all parts of the use of themselves: appearance, voice, movement, mannerisms, and accents. They also have excellent facility in playing characters from other places, times, and social strata, but most important, they are able to find the truth in the center of all the apparent differences between the character and themselves. They find where the character and themselves meet and meld.

Whether working within a broad or more narrow palette, emotional truthfulness and authenticity are always the actor's goal. But there are many ways into truth: through the emotions, imagination, and the body. Sometimes studying someone's walk and imitating it will give you immediate insight into that person. Adopting certain movement patterns, ways of using the body, and gestures (part of a person's use) can help you find the inmost truth of your character.

You may have certain habits or mannerisms that affect your use and get in the way of your acting. Sometimes these habits may actually work well for a character you are playing—other times, not so well. Occasionally, an actor becomes famous for a certain mannerism. Marlon Brando, for instance, was well known for his T-shirt, tight jeans, and mumbling speech pattern at a time when dressing smartly and speaking precisely were the norm among actors. Other young actors of the time started copying his way of dressing—and his mumbling—because this is easier to imitate than his genius! Brando himself demonstrated in several films, *Julius Caesar* in particular, that he could speak very well when he wanted to. You can follow Brando's example and choose when you want to alter something about yourself. That keeps your work exciting and fresh, variable, and surprising.

Postural Sets and Somaticizing

A postural set is a learned and remembered posture. We have certain ways of sitting, standing, walking, and doing all our physical activities. Your body anticipates how much muscle effort is necessary to maintain the posture associated with each activity. However, we're not static all the time, so we move from postural set to set—moving from sitting to standing to walking, for instance. Not everything about this is negative. It's positive in that you don't have to think about it every time you make one of these routine moves. What's not so positive is sometimes your body thinks it needs to work much harder than it actually does.

Becoming familiar with your habits and postural sets can be eye-opening. For instance, you can catch yourself slumping and collapsing each time your seat lowers onto a chair. Your body feels that the collapse is included in what sitting is supposed to be—collapsing is part of this "set," and your body "remembers" to collapse when you sit. But in a collapsed and pulled-down way of sitting, some muscles work too hard and some aren't working hard enough.

You also have a set for standing: you might slump down or put most of your weight on one leg and stick your hip out. You might have a personal set for walking. Some people jut their necks out and hunch their shoulders up toward their ears. You may lurch forward from your hips as you move forward through space. You may have "acting sets," such as habitual ways of holding sides to read at an audition. You may have a habitual way of standing or sitting that is overly tense when waiting to go into an audition. On the positive side, you can use various postural sets to help you define a character's physical life. That's one of the reasons why it can be so helpful for you to find how your character moves. The character's movement helps define the character's psychology.

To "somaticize" means to translate mental or emotional stress into the body. It can result in fatigue, loss of appetite, headaches, and gastrointestinal problems. Of course, almost no one does this on purpose. It can happen to anyone, and it can get in the way of your performing. It's completely understandable; performers are under intense pressure, and the body often reacts.

Sometimes the tensions of the character and your own personal tensions become confused. Rule number one of drama is *Drama is conflict*. The very thing we often try to avoid in real life is heightened in your professional life. Plays and films are full of all kinds of intense conflicts, even in comedy. Often, your character is supposed to be tense. How do you portray a tense character and not become so tense yourself that it closes down your body and voice, inhibiting your artistic expression? How do you not somaticize your character into your body when the play is over?

The answer is that you release the stress through your body into the life of the character. When you are balanced and free, you can *embody* the tension. You feel it, you experience it as is appropriate for your character, it moves through you, and that feeling is released out in the direction of the audience. It's a kind of energy flow through you and out to them. When you are doing this successfully, in a subtle and skillful way, this release of energy and emotion may feel cathartic to you. You have actually "lived the life of the character." You have thought, felt, and experienced life as she does—you have lived her conflicts truthfully. This is what a fully realized performance is.

It can help to use an image from Eastern philosophy. Think of your body, your self, as a hollow flute. When your instrument is in use, you allow air to move through you. You, as the performer, can allow all kinds of things to move through you. You have the power to let your imagination to go wild; and if it's your intention that you are a conduit, a hollow flute, nothing will get trapped inside you—it will be released and flow through you. It's a powerful feeling when it happens; very light and easy. It's even a little addictive. You'll want to do it again.

Body Image and Perfectionism

There are two other important elements to keep in mind: body image and perfectionism. Body image is an issue for everyone. We all seem to have feelings about our bodies and how they look. I hear students and others talk at length about their height, weight, body type, and how they feel about various parts of their bodies. Even actors who are sculpted from hours of working out often worry that they don't look good enough and are driven to work out longer and harder in an effort to look "perfect." We're also influenced by perfect images of perfect models with perfect retouching on the fronts of magazines and all over the Internet.

Performers feel more pressure than others to look their best at all times. Some people suck in their stomachs too hard, some men hold their arms artificially away from their bodies to make them look bigger, others slump down and pull their whole body in to try and make themselves look smaller. It's then very difficult to look at yourself objectively or consider how you might want to alter yourself physically to play a role. Many actors don't like looking in a mirror, or may be loath to dance in a musical, or may dread complex blocking in a farce partly because of the physicality that's involved.

How do you learn to like your body a little better? Or at least "accept" it as a start? How do you make peace with your body type? Always trying to make your body look better is one manifestation of *perfectionism*. One of the ironies of perfectionism is that it is a kind of tyranny that rules you and often gives you the opposite of what you want. Discipline and hard work are good; striving toward your best is good. But thinking that you will achieve physical perfection— and then freeze it forever—can turn you to stone. And thinking that you will "nail" the "perfect performance" every time can lead you into bad acting habits, tension, stiffness, a quality of constantly watching yourself, and a kind of ongoing dialogue with yourself about "How am I doing?" instead of just doing.

Abandon the idea of being able to create and completely control a "perfect performance" and focus instead on who the character is, what she wants, what she's going after—all these things should help bring you away from thoughts like "How do I look?" When you focus on the character, your mind-body will be looser, and so will your performance.

Distorting Yourself

Many actors want a job so badly they'll go into overdrive trying to figure out what "they" (producers, agents, casting directors) want and try to squeeze themselves into that little box. It's something for you to consider as you work on yourself—don't "follow the pack"; don't develop what used to be called herd instinct.

It's ironic that actors often follow a path that's unconventional compared with other parts of society, yet theater and film communities can sometimes lead people into a kind of "groupthink." That means the group reaches a consensus by "agreeing to agree." This dampens creativity and can wind up creating rigid rules that are often contradictory: "No one wants to see a revival." "People only want to see things they've seen before, but in a new way." "The best entertainment is family-friendly." "The only true art is when you take a risk." While it's good to consider the possible wisdom in any of these beliefs, it's also wise not to be overly swayed by them.

That's not to say you should automatically buck all trends and ignore the voices of experience that have been in the field for a long time. It's important to learn from others as well as from your own mistakes. But groupthink is hardly ever specific to the particular strengths or weaknesses of an individual. Be true to yourself and your talent, don't distort who you are, and be comfortable and confident in that. Adapt yourself to circumstances as necessary, but stay close to your core. In this way, you'll avoid overimitating other people—attempting to make the same acting choices they make or comparing your career choices to theirs.

The classic acting advice—"You can't compare your acting career to those of others; everyone has her own journey and trajectory"—is true. Whenever people compare too much, almost inevitably they end up feeling bad about their own choices. I'm confident that you can chart your own course with confidence in your own abilities as a serious artist. This will keep you more calm, comfortable, true to yourself, and freer in your mind-body and in your acting.

Lying

I don't see acting as a kind of lying. On the contrary, I see it as a type of truth-telling. But, like acting, lying is a complex mind-body activity, even in an exercise. It's challenging to execute without tightening up. In some sense, you're aware you are committing an act of subterfuge: you might feel a little guilty about it, and this may show itself in your body.

In this exercise, give yourself permission to do something slightly outrageous and still be balanced within yourself. Practice becoming "comfortable with your discomfort."

- You'll need a friend for this exercise.
- Tell your friend a series of deliberate lies.
- What happens in your body as you do this, especially in your head, neck, and shoulders?
- What do you notice about your breathing and your voice as you lie?
- Exaggerate your lies, and the manner in which you tell them. Be flamboyant.
- How does this affect your use?
- Now be quite subtle in your lies. Be as believable as possible.
- Have your friend tell you what she noticed about you as you lied.
- Switch roles. Have your friend go through the same lying sequence.
- What do you notice about your friend as she lies? About her body language? Her voice? Her manner, as she lies?

Subtext, or Irony

This exercise may initially feel a little unnatural to someone who is accustomed to speaking clearly, directly, and sincerely. It's still an excellent exercise. It's good to be able to communicate two opposing viewpoints at the same time while remaining poised within yourself. It's like juggling two balls, a baseball bat, and a toilet plunger. Keeps you on your game.

- Try this exercise with a friend.
- Choose a simple sentence or short paragraph and say it, meaning the opposite. For instance say, "I'm really looking forward to going to the party."

- Don't be obvious in your intent. Attempt to be sincere. But inside, in your thoughts, know that you mean the opposite.
- Try saying several sentences, meaning the opposite, deep inside.
- What do you notice in your body, your breathing, and your feelings as you do this?
- Switch roles and have your partner do the same thing.
- What do you notice about her as she is unintentionally ironic?

Trying too Hard in Daily Life

Trying too hard is one of the primary things that causes stress and tension. The irony is, when you're trying too hard, you're attempting to help yourself—but you're actually hurting yourself. This exercise helps you to feel that more clearly in your body in everyday activities.

- Take hold of a pen and bear down hard as you write. Write fast. What happens to your hands, wrists, arms? Your whole torso?
- Pretend you have an intense deadline and need to write an important e-mail. Type hard and fast on the computer. What happens in your hands, arms, and torso? Even your legs and breathing may be affected.
- Get a jar with a tight lid from the kitchen. Try to open it. What happens with your body? Your breathing? Exaggerate your habits so you can feel them more clearly.
- Next time you are in the shower, notice how you wash your hair. How are you using the soap on your body?
- Pay attention when you are brushing your teeth. If you sense yourself grabbing the toothbrush too hard and tensing your arm, increase the effort even more and feel what that feels like.
- Go up and down a flight of stairs. What do you notice about your neck, shoulders, and lower back? If you're not sure what's happening, put your hand there, and keep it relaxed as you go up the stairs. This will help you feel what's happening in that area. Increase your level of effort so you feel what your habit is.
- Go up onto your toes to reach something off a high shelf. Do you arch your lower back? Tense your shoulders and lift them toward your ears? Hold your breath? Go ahead—do it even more so you get a sense of it.

Being Yourself

This is a deceptively easy exercise. You just lie there for several minutes and think about letting go. What's the big deal? For many people, it's quite a big deal to allow themselves to be who they are. For all kinds of reasons, sometimes unconsciously, they may have felt it necessary to force themselves into certain ways of presenting themselves to the world. They may have felt it necessary to have certain thoughts, ideas, and feelings; to wear certain types of clothes; to speak a certain way; and to hold their bodies and move a certain way. I'm suggesting that for a relatively short period of time you attempt to put that all aside as much as possible and reconnect with your quiet core. Listen to the still voice inside that is you as opposed to who you may have thought you "should" be in the past. Don't be surprised if some feelings come up. Remind yourself that you're in a safe space and that if the feelings do come up, it's okay.

- Sit quietly in a chair, or lie down on the floor with a paperback book under your head, knees bent, and hands on your rib cage.
- Sense your own breathing.
- Allow your breath to be easy.
- Let yourself sigh a few times.
- See if you can let yourself be in the moment and not be too concerned with the past few days or what's coming up soon.
- Stay with a sense of your own body, and your own breathing.
- If thoughts come into your mind, allow them to pass through, then return to your calm focus.
- See if you can enjoy being in your body for a few minutes, and enjoy not "being in activity," but just being.
- *Let your neck be free, to let your torso lengthen and widen, your arms and legs to release away from the body.*
- Just be quiet in yourself.
- Breathe out easily.

Somaticizing

Tension and stress have to go somewhere in the mind and body—unless they are "processed." If tension and stress are processed successfully, you won't have to lodge them in your muscles through spasms and knots in what has been called *body armoring*. Once you start thinking about the simple concept, you'll begin to catch yourself holding tension and stress all the time. When you catch yourself, you can return to home base by reminding yourself to release as much as possible and not go into old, destructive habits. Being aware of your thoughts and feelings, and of the tightness and holdings in your body, is all the processing you need to do.

- Spread out some paper out on a table and have a pencil ready.
- Sit comfortably and prepare yourself by releasing your body and breathing. Think through your Alexander thoughts.
- Look at the blank paper.
- Now imagine the outline of your own body.
- Draw your experience of the outline of your own body. It doesn't have to look exactly like what you look like; let it represent what you feel like.
- Pause and think about where you feel pain, tension, or restriction.
- Sketch those things inside your body. Draw it the way you feel it.
- Take a look at how your body looks—where tension and pain tend to congregate. Does it tend to be mostly on one side? Or in one area of the body? How does it make your body feel? Fatigued? Tight? Heavy?
- Now draw an idealized self—lighter, easier, and freer. Less pain and restriction.
- What does that look like? How does it make you feel?
- What would it be like to have that sense of yourself more often?

Hollow Flute

The central metaphor of this activity is simple, and it helps to unlock all the tensions that tend to creep into your body unnoticed. The image of hollowness in yourself helps to clear out the holdings throughout your body.

This idea of allowing something to move through you helps you prepare for the strong emotions that have to flow through you in performance: anger, pain, regret, fury, bitterness, and so on—these are sometimes uncomfortable emotions we try to avoid in daily life but are often front and center in a play or film. After an intense performance, this practical exercise will help you to gradually release and let go of that strong emotion.

- Lie down on the floor, a paperback book under your head.
- Since you'll be here awhile, place your lower legs on top of a chair or ottoman to support them.

- Place your hands on your lower rib cage.
- Allow your body to fall back on the floor, without pushing it.
- Think your flow concepts: *Let the neck be free, to let the head be balanced at the end of the spine, to let the torso lengthen and widen.*
- Let your breathing be free, flowing in and out easily.
- Allow your mind and emotions to be quiet and calm.
- Let your body be easy.
- Imagine that your body is full of air.
- Sense the lightness in your body.
- Visualize that your body is hollow, like a tube or a flute.
- Imagine that air can move through you from top to bottom.
- Now visualize a color moving through you from head to toe.
- If you like, you can imagine sensations moving through you: heat, cold, a prickliness, a smoothness, whatever sensation you like.
- Return to "neutral." The calm, quiet center.
- Breathe low and slow.

Antiperfectionism

This exercise is close to my heart. As a reformed perfectionist, I understand the issue well. Perfectionism seems to be hardwired at a young age and there's no doubt that you often get rewarded for this kind of behavior, especially in school. Perfectionists are often hard workers, disciplined, self-motivated, and often persistent. But if you take it too far, sometimes you can't get started on projects because you are so concerned about making every detail "just right."

The whole concept of "perfection" is somewhat of a fiction—it doesn't really exist. To lift the burden of perfectionism off your shoulders can be surprisingly liberating. It's a process, and happens gradually, since it's a long-standing way of being. But you'll come to see that you can be much more spontaneous and inventive in your acting work when this well-meaning propensity for trying to "get it right" fades and a predisposition toward "exploring the creative unknown" takes over. It will open up your acting horizons in unforeseen ways if you can "embrace the mistakes."

- Take out your mind-body journal.
- Write down whether or not you feel you have perfectionist tendencies.
- Make a list of what your perfectionist tendencies might be: physical, mental, emotional, and so on.

- If you feel you aren't a perfectionist yourself, choose another actor you know that you feel may be. Write about her. (Don't tell your colleague you wrote about her! It might offend her.)
- Think about the list. What do you feel might be negative consequences of these habits?
- Note how perfectionism might affect your mind-body emotions.
- Make a list of how you might soften some of your overly scrupulous ways.
- List the personal benefits of not being a perfectionist.
- Are there one or two small scrupulous habits you could begin to alter that might help your acting? What are they? When and how could you begin to work on them?
- Make a list of actors or people in the public eye that you feel are not overly careful or perfectionists. What makes you think that? And what are the benefits for them, and for their audience?

5

Changing Your Mind-Body

Sometimes it's tempting to break your life into discrete segments and attempt to put distance between your real life and acting. But of course you want to bring real life into your acting to make it as natural as possible, and you want to bring some of your acting focus and acuteness into your day-to-day life. One helps the other, and they encourage each other to grow, art and life together.

Does this sound familiar? In your normal everyday life, you walk down the street and see someone unique who catches your eye. You observe, soak up details about that person, and make a mental note to remember a walk, a hat, the way a bag was carried—because you can "use that" for a character. You don't know which character yet, so you store the information away in your mind. These instinctive "actor experiences" somehow teach you about people, psychology, and human behavior. The whole sequence may take a few minutes, possibly less. You carry out this type of acting work almost without thinking about it as you conduct your regular activities.

You can also work on yourself psycho-physically throughout the day as you go about your business. Thinking the Alexander thoughts is simpler than checking in and out of social media. With just a few minutes here and there several times a day, you can work on your body, breathing, voice, emotional life—creating a multiplatform self-improvement program that will be abundantly useful to you in the moment, invaluable to your acting life, and aid you in prudently storing your experiences away for future use to create unique and authentic performances.

Changing the use of yourself in daily life is doable. It's not overwhelming to think about altering how you hold a coffee cup, bend over to pick something up off the floor, or get dressed in the morning. These are all comprehensible. Ultimately, you're working to increase your self-awareness, which is very different than being self-conscious. Self-conscious means feeling awkward and being afraid of making a mistake. Self-aware is the opposite. Under the best of circumstances, it means that you are poised, in the flow of things, and in the periphery of your focus you are cognizant of your body, emotions, and thoughts—without any of this overwhelming you in any way. Applying an improved use of yourself is also possible in your acting life.

Using Yourself as a Finely Tuned Instrument

Think of yourself almost as though you were an expensive violin. All you have to do is barely touch the bow against the strings, and it responds. This dynamic also holds true each time you run your fingers across the screen of a phone or tablet and the device responds your command. You have the impulse; the instrument responds. The Alexander Technique works in the same way: when you *think* an Alexander suggestion (impulse), you want your body to follow and respond subtly and effectively (response). You are designed to work this way and, as with any theatrical endeavor, your impulse and response get easier and better with practice. The more you think through the Alexander concepts, the more your muscles and nervous system will respond, with no need to force the issue. Your thinking is enough to guide you.

Before you give yourself suggestions of what you want, there is the all-important step of poise, or suspension. It's difficult to emphasize the importance of this step strongly enough. Without pausing, most likely you will return to your ingrained habits. With conscious suspension, you give yourself the chance to do something new. It takes repetition, because habit is so stubborn and it will try to jump right in each time.

Imagine your habit is like an enthusiastic dog who keeps trying to chew on your slippers. It serves you best if you calmly but firmly tell your dog (your habit) no and then give instructions for what you do want ("Don't chew on my slippers, please!"). In your own body, you may catch yourself tightening your neck. You tell yourself gently, "No, I don't want to do that. Instead, I'd like my neck muscles to release." Then you trust that the message will travel from your brain through to your muscular system. It's like sending an e-mail. You send it; it's received. There's no need to "hold on to" this thought. Holding on leads to tightening and stiffening.

Optimism versus the Alternative

In terms of both acting and everyday life, I would say that I'm a pragmatic optimist (to coin a phrase). Pragmatism means doing what works and developing your theories out of your own experience. Alexander himself was a pragmatist, as was his famous student John Dewey, the educator and philosopher. This belief system can trace its development back to America in the 1870s, to the philosophers William James and Charles Sanders Peirce, who wrote the aptly titled "How to Make Our Ideas Clear." My interpretation of optimism doesn't mean I believe we are living in (to quote *Candide*) "the best of all possible worlds." Rather, I choose to "make the best of what we have." While we may have limited influence over the world at large, we have a great deal of influence over the functioning of ourselves.

The following quotation, from an article on the subject of optimism and pessimism written by a team of psychologists, sums up my approach: "Optimists seem intent on facing problems head-on, taking active and constructive steps to solve their problems; pessimists are more likely to abandon their effort to attain their goals." This general attitude helps me greatly in my Alexander teaching and my acting.

In addition to working with actors, dancers, singers, and public speakers, I also work with people who suffer from neck and back pain, dystonia (a movement disorder that causes severe muscle spasms), and Parkinson's disease. Sometimes the people I see have to deal with very difficult symptoms on a daily basis. Yet my attitude is always, "Let's see if we can help you feel better, right here, right now." Even in cases where there is tremendous acute pain, there is usually something that can be done to make it at least a little bit better. I call this my *two-percent* rule. I can usually get someone to feel at least two percent better. Then I try to get two percent more, and two percent more—to build on that change. Before you know it, you have a ten percent improvement in a relatively short time, which is significant. You don't have to be an optimist to practice the Alexander Technique, but it's good to remind yourself that sometimes things *can*, and *do*, get better. Sometimes they improve quite a bit.

When a friend of mine turned thirty, he said, "That's it. My body just isn't what it used to be." He felt the rest of his life was going to be a slow slide and decline. I said, "Don't you think it's a little early to feel this way? Aren't you too young to start reminiscing about the good old days?" Whatever a person's age, I firmly believe that being actively engaged in the moment, having things to look forward to, and not being locked into the past give people a refreshing and vigorous approach to life. Some of the "youngest" people I know are in their eighties and nineties, because of their unconventional, optimistic approach to life. We can all learn something from them, especially if someone of that age is more freethinking than we are!

These people chart their own courses. They've made definite choices in their lives. Some of them decided, in their eighties, to study the Alexander Technique. They just didn't accept the idea that learning stops somewhere earlier in life. They are committed to the concept of lifelong learning and follow the holistic idea that we each can take responsibility for our own psycho-physical health. It's very freeing when you find out that you are in charge of your own life and that no one is going to breathe down your neck to get you to do things.

Taking Responsibility for Your Choices

Eleanor Roosevelt once said, "In the long run, we shape our lives, and we shape ourselves. The process never ends until we die. And the choices we make are ultimately our own responsibility."

This quotation has great relevance for actors: after all, a career as an actor is a choice you are making. This is what you want to do. You are your own small business, and *the work is its own reward*—that's a phrase to remember. If you adopt this approach, it will help you keep your equilibrium more easily. And it's important to remember that you can change your course at any time you want. If you want to go in a different direction, you can. You are the one in charge of your own life.

No matter how challenging things may get professionally, it almost never helps to get frantic or desperate. Keeping a warm heart and a cool head may help you through some tricky situations, but it will also help you when a rush of success comes your way. Success goes straight to some people's heads, so you'll want to keep your feet firmly on the ground, whether things are going badly or tremendously.

The Alexander principles can be a practical help in constructively "staying with yourself" instead of getting pulled in all directions by outside forces. It's certainly possible to be the calm center of the storm that is a life in the performing arts. There can be all kinds of frenetic activity around you, but you can stand firm when you need to and sway in the wind when necessary. If you're balanced inside yourself, you'll know what to do. You'll stick with what you do best, and who you are, steering your own course in the midst of your life in the performing arts.

PART ONE: Everyday Movements

The Daily Tune-In—Catching Yourself Midstream

This is one of the most central exercises, if not *the* most central exercise, in this book. It bears repeating over and over. Because we are all such creatures of habit, and our habits get in our way numerous times a day, it benefits us to counteract those tensions through reminding ourselves of our process instructions. This exercise is nonjudgmental. You are not out to admonish yourself into altering how you function. If anything, I'd suggest the opposite approach. When you catch yourself doing something unconstructive, rather than saying, "Stop doing that now!" you say something along the lines of, "Isn't that interesting? Look at what I'm doing here. I wonder why I'm doing that. Let me think how I can work with myself to bring about a change." I would call this almost a gentle and laid-back scientific approach. Give it a try and see how it works for you.

- In the middle of whatever you are doing, "tune in" or "drop in" on yourself.
- Don't change anything, just observe.
- Ask yourself, what's happening with my body? What general position am I in? What's happening with my neck and head? Is my neck stiff or tight? Is it pulling forward, or pulled to one side? Is my head retracted back, pushing down onto my neck?
- Are your shoulders lifted or rolled forward? Is your torso hunched over, or overly tight? What's happening in your legs, your arms, and your hands?
- Be aware of your breathing. Is it held or too shallow?
- How would you describe your body overall, at this moment?
- Do you often find yourself this way?
- Take a moment to pause, and remind yourself consciously that you'd like to change how you do things.
- To help you release, think through your Alexander process instructions: *Let your neck be free, to let your torso lengthen and widen, to let your arms and legs release away from your torso. Think your shoulders and chest open.*
- Rather than allowing yourself to collapse or pull down, think up and out.
- Continue with whatever you are doing.

Sitting at the Computer

Without a doubt, sitting at the computer (or, I should say, hunching at the computer) for hours at a time is one of the most challenging tasks of contemporary life. But shouldn't you be sovereign over your computer? A recent cartoon showed evolution as a gradual progression from ape to fully standing human, to a gradual regression into rounding over into an ape position again, with the human sitting in front of a tablet computer!

There seem to be a number of factors that bring about the "computer hunch": the chair you sit on, the height of the computer, how the computer is set up on the desk or tabletop, the height of the working surface, the amount of work light available, and last but most important—*how* you are sitting and using yourself in this work environment. Also, what's on the screen seems to pull us toward it with almost magnetic force. We want to be closer to what we are looking at and what we are writing. Your neck juts forward; your head retracts back. Sometimes you squint—I won't even mention glasses and how they figure into the equation.

Challenging, but all solvable problems. You can improve your work area to make it function better for you. Keep your main objective in mind: to allow yourself to gently lengthen into your full stature as you sit working at the computer. If you need to move forward to see something on the screen, try leaning in from your hips rather than breaking at your waist. Monitor yourself to see that you're not tightening in your wrists and forearms as you type, and keep the breathing flowing. Take breaks as often as you can. Stand and stretch, even if it's just for a moment, every thirty minutes if you can.

- Sit and work at the computer as you do normally.
- Give your attention to how you are using your body.
- Do you pull your body toward the computer?
- What's happening in your shoulders, arms, and hands as you type?
- What is your general body position as you work?
- What's happening with your head and neck?
- How does your breathing function here at the computer?
- If you work on multiple screens, or go back and forth between e-mail, social media, documents, and texts—watch what you do.
- Keep typing as you remind yourself that you'd like to alter how you work at the computer.
- Think through the Alexander thoughts. Keep your breathing easy and free.

Texting and Working on a Tablet

The phone and tablet's strong points are also their weak points in terms of posture. Their small size allows wonderful portability, but they also tend to encourage users to hunch over when typing on them, especially when texting. Unconsciously, people round over quite far to get closer to the small screen and to concentrate on their messages. Sometimes the typing is not accurate, which makes people tense even more. Tablets are easier to use because they are larger and more sensitive to the touch, but they can be challenging to balance as you move about. One of the simplest and most effective things you can do is alter the position of your device: raise it up higher, remember to lengthen upward, and remain at a comfortable distance from it. It's helpful to remember "back and up" as a direction as opposed to "forward and down" toward your device.

- The next time you text, check what you do with your body.
- What level do you hold the device at? Can you see it easily?
- What do you do with your arms and hands as you text?
- How does your breathing function during this activity?
- Do you walk and text at the same time? How is that working for you?
- Where is your torso, generally, as you text?
- Are your shoulders squeezing together?
- Do your neck and head pull down to the device?
- Are you able to hold the device higher so you don't cave over so far?
- Think through your Alexander thoughts and keep your breath easy as you continue to text.

Speaking on the Phone

I'm assuming you spend most of your phone time on a cell phone. If you do use a landline, that has its own challenges—mainly, not resting the receiver on your shoulder and craning your neck over to hold it there while you're doing other things. With a cell phone there are other things to keep in mind. A commonsense solution is to use earbuds or the speakerphone if you are on the phone for long periods or if you are making many calls. It's helpful to remember to "go up," or think of lengthening yourself, as you are speaking. Over time you will associate this with being on the phone, and you'll have less of a tendency to pull down to the phone. Bring the phone up to yourself rather than yourself to the phone.

- "Tune in" to yourself as you speak on the phone.
- Do you use earbuds or the speakerphone?
- How do you use your phone in relation to your body? How does your body adjust to it?
- Do you walk and talk on the phone often? How is that working for you?

- Are you on social media or the computer as you're on the phone? How are you managing that?
- Do you speak on the phone as you drive? What does your body do as you do that?
- Does your body tend to pull down toward the phone, especially if you're having trouble hearing or the call is breaking up?
- Think your Alexander thoughts, and see what happens when you allow upward energy to flow through you. How does that affect the activity?
- Are you able to stay wide across your shoulders and chest as you are on the phone?
- Can you keep your breathing easy?

Walking

Walking is one of our most basic and important movements, yet so often we take it for granted. It's "just my walk," people say. An upright walk is what separates humans from other mammals. Under ideal circumstances, it is almost a miracle of motion. At its most sophisticated, this series of minute and complex micromovements gives the impression that one has continuous, flowing *motility* (the ability to move spontaneously and actively). Changing your walk, handwriting, and voice are three of the hardest things you can do because they feel so personal. The sense of "who we are" seems to be very tied up with how we walk, write, and speak. Because of this, it takes finesse when beginning to change your walk. It can feel odd at first, and you may miss certain aspects of your old walk—even the tension! Somehow the tension can feel like it "stabilizes" your body as it moves, but you will soon see that the best stabilizer of a body in motion is balance. And one of the most effective ways of helping you to define a character, both for yourself and for the audience, is to find that character's walk.

- "Drop in" on yourself and sense how you walk when you're walking on the street or at home.
- Check your head-neck balance. Do you tend to pull your neck forward when you walk, or pull your head back and down?
- Be aware of your shoulders and torso.
- Do your arms swing naturally as you walk? If you carry a bag or backpack, how does your body accommodate that?

- What happens in your legs? Do you walk coming down onto your heel and roll through your whole foot, or do you walk flat-footed? Are your toes overly turned out or in?
- Do you tend to glide when you walk? Or come down heavily on your feet? Does one foot hit the ground more heavily than the other?
- How would you describe your walk overall? Heavy, light, smooth, uneven, lurching, efficient, or inefficient?
- Does the energy in your body tend to go down toward the ground or up toward the sky when you walk?
- Think through the flow thoughts, to help you move more easily. *Let the neck be free, the torso to lengthen and widen* as you move.
- Keep your breath flowing.
- Allow your shoulders and hips to move gently as you walk. This gives almost a massaging action to your back.

Moving In and Out of a Chair

Standing and sitting—what could be more simple? The simplicity is actually an illusion. A series of complex and interrelated motions throughout your whole body is needed to bring you up and down into a chair. Observe someone who is very advanced in age, or someone who has a physical challenge, and note the difficulty with which that person performs this action. In addition, there is the trajectory (angle) of the motion to be considered, the height and shape of the chair, and whether or not you are using momentum (largely determined by the speed with which you move). As with walking, the habits associated with sitting are strong, largely because we do it so often and with so little thought.

- Stand up from a chair without thinking too much about it.
- Sit down in your usual way.
- See if you notice anything about how you move. Try this a few times.
- Keeping your hands released, place them on the back of your neck. Stand and sit several times. What do you feel in your neck as you do this?
- Leaving your hands easy, place them on your shoulders. Stand and sit several times and see what you notice.
- Place your hands on your midsection, near your waist. Stand and sit a few times. What do you observe?

- Imagine that you are very tired. Stand and sit a few times. What happens in your body? Do you drop yourself into the chair? Does your body get more heavy?
- Sit in the chair the way you would when you've been sitting for some time, either in front of the computer or watching television. Is there a downward pull or collapse through your torso?
- Sensing this downward energy in your body, see how much effort it takes to bring yourself out of the chair. What do you do with your body under these circumstances?
- Sit in the chair and ask yourself not to pull down. Think through the Alexander thoughts: *Let your neck be free, to let your head go forward and up, to let your torso lengthen and widen.*
- In sitting, move back and forward from your hip joints rather than from your waist. Your back remains lengthened as you move.
- Have both your feet on the floor, close to the chair. Staying lengthened, let your head come over your feet, straighten your legs to come up out of the chair.
- Try the reverse: stand with your torso gently lengthened. Bend at your ankles, knees, and hips to lower yourself down into the chair. It's an easy, controlled motion.

Carrying Things

All actors have bags. Rehearsal clothes, costumes, laptops, phones, scripts, props, food—this is a lot of stuff, and you cart it around. Carrying heavy things can be one of the contributing factors in neck and shoulder tension, especially those places at the base of your neck and the top of your shoulders where "rocks" can take up residence. Bringing your awareness to this issue is a big step, as is changing where you place your bag and how you carry it. Also, it helps to find a bag that works for you. I highly recommend taking everything out of your bag that isn't absolutely necessary, especially if you're toting it around all day. It may help to have a couple of different bags, so you're not always putting pressure on the same places in your body. But most important of all is working *with* gravity rather than *against* it, because gravity will win every time. Thinking up through your body as a counterweight to the downward pressure of the bag is a back saver. It's almost like you're a piece of elastic that is gently stretching in two directions: the torso lengthens up, the legs lengthen down.

- Observe yourself carrying a bag, backpack, or heavy suitcase.
- Be aware of the weight of the bags.
- Which side do you carry the bag on? Do you ever switch your bag from one shoulder to the other? Do you ever put the strap of your bag on one shoulder and have the strap cross your body diagonally?
- How does your body react to the bag and the weight? Do you tend to pull down toward the bag or away from it?
- If you are wearing a backpack, do you tend to hunch forward to counterbalance the weight on your back? Do your shoulders roll forward? How is your neck?
- If you pull a rolling bag, is the handle long enough? Do you lean over as you wheel the bag?
- If carrying something fairly heavy in front of you (a baby, or groceries, for instance), try carrying it as close to you as possible, near your center of gravity.
- Whatever you are carrying, there is a downward pressure from the weight of the load. Rather than allowing your body to be pulled down with the bag, sense the weight of the bag. Also be aware of your body releasing up away from the ground as a positive counterbalance.
- Note what happens when you carry something in front of you, especially if it is heavy. Does your upper back lean back, and are you arching your lower back? Rather than breaking yourself in two, think of allowing your whole body to lean slightly back from your ankles to counterbalance. That way your whole body stays in one piece.
- Think through your Alexander thoughts: *Neck free, head forward and up, torso lengthening and widening.* Let your breathing be free.
- Allow your body to lengthen up, even with the downward weight coming from the bags.

Bending, Reaching, and Lifting

When bending forward, many people hunch, dropping the neck and shoulders forward. This is not efficient for the body, especially in reaching and lifting. High-performing athletes, on the other hand—including tennis players, baseball players, and golfers—adopt a healthier way of bending, what's called a *position of mechanical advantage*. In this position, the knees are bent and the body leans forward from the hips in an elongated stance. You can use this stance in many situations, especially when lifting or moving heavy objects.

To find your hip sockets, stand comfortably. Shift your weight onto your left leg, bend your right knee forward, and pick your right foot up off the floor.

Bring your knee to a ninety-degree angle in front of you. Place your hand at the juncture where your leg and torso meet. That's the hip socket. You can also check it out online at an anatomy website or app. The hip socket is where you are designed to bend.

Your body is in a very strong and flexible stance while in a position of mechanical advantage; you're ready to move, to use force if necessary. Bending and lifting this way will protect your back and prevent injuries. Consider it the next time you need to lift another actor in a production!

- Notice how you bend to pick something up off a coffee table or the floor.
- Where do you bend from?
- What happens with your head, neck, and shoulders as you bend? Does your head retract back and down?
- Do you hold your breath when you reach for something?
- How do you take hold of the object? Do you grasp with a lot of effort in your hands and arms?
- Think through your Alexander directions.
- While continuing to think of lengthening your torso, try bending your knees forward and leaning forward from your hip sockets rather than from your waist. Your torso remains lengthened as you move.
- Try this at the bathroom and kitchen sinks.
- Try picking up objects from a coffee table or the floor in this way. It's not just a matter of "bending your knees." It's *how* you are bending your knees—moving from your hips rather than your waist and using your body as a unit.
- If you lift something heavy from the floor, follow the standard advice of bending your knees, but also leave your torso lengthened and engage your lower core muscles in your abdomen to protect your back.
- What happens when you reach up for something—in a closet, for instance? Or when you wash your hair in the shower, do your shoulders lift up or roll forward? Does your lower back arch? See what happens when you think your Alexander thoughts.

Lunging

Lunging simply means bending one knee when the other leg is straight. Usually, the front leg is bent and the back leg is straight. But it can be the reverse. You can also lunge to the side. Lunging is another powerful position of mechanical advantage. It can feel a little odd at first, since most of us are so used to collapsing or pulling down in our midsections when we lean over. But once you practice it a bit, it can feel quite strong and pleasurable.

Lunging is similar to some of the motions in tai chi or fencing. Using the lunge when you're doing things around the house or yard can help to strengthen your middle and lower back and core muscles. Also, if you trip and lose your balance, you'll have a better chance of keeping yourself from falling if you take a lunging step. This motion also gives you a strong sense of your center of gravity around the pelvis. The more you lunge, the more connected you will be with your center. You will also be able to bring that connection with you into other movements.

- Are you ever in a lunging position? You may come close to it when vacuuming, sweeping, mopping the floor, or raking.
- Check to see if you collapse at your waist and squeeze down through your midsection when doing any of these activities.
- Recall your Alexander thoughts: *Neck free, head forward and up, torso lengthening and widening.*
- Try leaning forward from your hip joints rather than your waist.
- There are many applications for lunging. Try picking something up off a coffee table or a low bookcase in a lunge.
- It's safer for your back to move a heavy piece of furniture in a lunge. Your back stays lengthened, you have a lower center of gravity, and you'll move the object using the large muscles of the back rather than just your shoulders and neck.

Using the Stairs

The tendency, both in going up and down the stairs, is to pull down. When going down the stairs, you can often hear a heaviness when you clomp down the stairs, even if the steps are carpeted. You might also have an unconscious fear of falling when coming down the stairs, gripping the banister with your hand and forearm and dropping your head and neck forward to see where you are going. It may be counterintuitive, but you can find easier balance through staying at your full height, and just tipping your head forward to see where you are going. The top of your spine is between your ears, behind your nose: that's the point to tip from. When going up the stairs, aim not to hike yourself up with your back muscles or yank yourself up with your arm and shoulder on the banister. Trust that your body coordination and your direction of thinking up will help you move up the stairs without undue effort.

- Observe yourself as you use the stairs.
- Do you hunch forward or arch your lower back as you go up the stairs? Are you unconsciously trying to lift yourself up the stairs with your back rather than using your legs?
- Do you grip the banister tightly?
- When you come down the stairs, are you heavy on your feet?
- Do you pull your neck forward to see where you are going?
- When going up or down the stairs, allow yourself to *think up* rather than compressing the body down.
- When going up the stairs, see if you can refrain from pulling your head back and down as you look up.
- Direct yourself to remain lengthened as you go down the stairs. You don't need to crane your neck to see the stairs. Leave your neck lengthened and tip your head from the top of your spine, in between your ears, to look down.
- With each step up or down, let that be a gentle reminder to *go up* within yourself. Let your legs do most of the work, and let your torso go along for the ride.

Eating

It's sometimes not easy for people to change how they eat. But putting some thought into it can help make eating easier on the body. Like the computer and mobile devices, food is placed down and in front of a person—but having everything in that position may make you susceptible to pulling forward and down toward your food. By staying *back and up*, and suggesting an upward flow through your musculature, you will reduce your body's habit of curling toward your food. See what it's like to take your time when eating, tasting your food, engaging in conversation, and noticing your surroundings.

- Eat as you do normally.
- As you are eating, give your attention to how you do it, without changing anything.
- Do you hunch over, to get closer to your food?
- Are your shoulders pulled forward, toward your food?
- Is your torso hunched over toward the table?
- What happens to your breathing as you eat?

- If you are dining with someone, how do you manage physically as you are eating and talking?
- Continue eating as you consciously decide to take another approach. Keep eating as you think through the Alexander instructions.
- If you need to lean forward toward your food, lean from your hip joints rather than from your waist. As you lean forward, keep your body lengthened.
- Bring your food all the way up to your mouth rather than bringing your body down to your food. It may feel different at first.
- Rather than pulling your body down when you drink, bring the glass all the way up to your mouth and tip the head gently back from the top of the spine, in between your ears.

PART TWO: Expanding Yourself Through Movement

Walking Backward

You don't often walk backward more than a few steps, so you have few habits associated with this motion. It makes your brain work in a slightly different way. Sometimes walking backward helps *bring you into your back*, meaning it lengthens your back and helps to prevent overarching. People often "walk taller" when they walk backward. Your body learns from this, and you're more able to maintain length when you return to walking forward. In addition, when walking forward your walk is heel-toe: your heel comes onto the ground first, you roll through your foot, and push off with your toes going down into the ground, which helps to bring your knee forward. When walking backwards your toes come onto the ground first, then the heel. Be sensitive with your feet as you walk this way. It will help make the action easier.

- Think of lengthening and widening, and allow your breath to flow in and out.
- Put your hands on your lower rib cage. Allow your ribs to move in and out.
- After making sure there's nothing behind you, slowly walk backwards.
- Check to make sure you don't hold your breath; let your ribs move.
- Continue thinking up.

- See if you can allow your back to be more sensitive than usual. Can your back almost "see" where you are going?
- Be aware through your whole body as you move backward through space.
- Watch that your focus is not making you hold your breath or making your breath shallow.
- Try exhaling as you walk backward to help renew your psycho-physical freedom.

Speaking as You Walk

Coordinating the actions of walking, breathing, and speaking easily is a type of theatrical multitasking. Every actor needs to know how to do it. Finding freedom in this will also aid you in freeing yourself technically, thus allowing your emotions to come through more easily. It's like an opera singer learning how to scream when her character is killed. First, she learns technically how to scream without hurting her voice. Then when she screams in performance, she can give herself over to the emotion of the scream. When you find the flow of movement, combined with easy breathing and speech, it will allow you to let yourself fly in performance and focus on what you are saying and feeling, trusting that the movement and vocal production will be there to support you.

- Think up as you breathe easily.
- Walk forward several steps, then backward. Keep your breath flowing.
- Count to five as you walk forward, count to five as you walk backwards.
- Check to see that you're not making your breath shallow.
- Try counting two sets of five as you walk forward and backward.
- Use the cross-pattern reflex. If your right foot comes forward, your left arm comes forward. The left foot moves with the right arm.
- This promotes diagonal stretches up the front and back of your torso. This, together with your free breathing, gives an almost massaging effect on your back, especially your lower back.
- Allow the hips to move gently. Don't keep them overly still. This is their natural movement.
- Count to five, three sets walking forward and three sets walking backward. Note what happens to you when you do this.

Soft Eyes

Focusing on releasing your eyes and the muscles around your eyes has so many applications. Alexander said that if someone was fixed or glazed in her eyes, there was no possibility for release anywhere else in the body. I've found the opposite is also true: if you release your eyes, it helps your whole body to let go. It's especially challenging to allow your eyes to stay easy when you are focusing your attention on something deeply. Once you are able to do that, it will help your acting to become more natural and organic. It's especially important to be released in your face and eyes when doing on-camera work.

- Stand or sit comfortably.
- Think through the Alexander process suggestions: *Let your neck be free, to let your head go forward and up…*
- Tune in to your breathing.
- Exhale three times.
- Give your attention to your eyes and the muscles around your eyes.
- What do you notice about them? What is your sense of them, the muscles of the eyebrows, in between the eyebrows, underneath, and to the sides of the eyes? The eyes themselves?
- Close your eyes.
- Place your palms over your eyes. This helps to bring real darkness, to help your eyes release. It's called *palming*.
- Ask yourself to release your eyes. And all the muscles around your eyes. The darkness will help this happen.
- Allow your breath to be easy.
- Take your palms down, and let your eyes open.
- Let your eyes be soft and open.
- Don't "try to see." Let whatever you're looking at "come to you."
- Continuing with the idea of having a soft focus, look from one side of the room to the other.
- Let your eyes be soft as you look down the floor, and up to the ceiling.
- Say a speech you know, or read a piece of text. See if you can keep your eyes released, open, and undefended.
- Begin to use this idea in scene study or rehearsals.

Shifting Weight

Shifting your weight is something you do all the time, without thinking about it. But if you begin to think about it, your balance will become more refined.

Often when people shift their weight, there's a whole series of unnecessary tensions that are set off, almost like a domino effect. The body feels like it needs to tighten in several places to keep from losing balance or falling. These tensions are attempting to stabilize you. However, if you can stabilize yourself through balance, you will move much more efficiently. Continuing to *release up* throughout the shifting movement prevents you from pulling down and stops your shoulders and hips from going off-kilter. This is important in walking, running, going up stairs, and in many other activities.

- Stand with your weight balanced evenly over your two feet.
- *Think up* along your spine.
- Exhale three times.
- Shift your weight onto your right foot.
- Check to see that your hips stay even.
- Stay elongated up both sides of your body, so you don't pull down either side.
- Shift your weight onto your left foot.
- Shift your weight back and forth several times, leaving your body poised as you do so. Check to make sure you don't pull down either side.
- Leave your breath easy.
- Maintain your balance as you shift.

Standing on One Foot

This takes the shift of weight a step further. When standing on one leg, in addition to lengthening and not pulling down, your body will execute many micromovements in your foot, ankle, leg, and whole body to remain balanced. When integrated with your breathing, this is a very healthy exercise to build strength, coordination, and balance.

- Stand comfortably. Place one of your hands lightly on the back of a chair to help maintain your balance. Think your Alexander thoughts.
- From a neutral stance, shift your weight onto your right foot.
- Bend your left knee and lift it up in front of you.
- Stand balanced on your right leg. Check to see that you don't pull to one side or the other. Note that your hips stay even.
- Stand poised in this manner for several seconds.
- Bring your foot down. Remember to think up.
- Shift your weight, and stand on your left foot.

- Bend your right knee and lift it up in front of you.
- Stay easy in yourself as you balance. Breathe freely.
- Repeat on both sides.

Rounding Over

The full rounding over of your spine is probably not an activity you do often— that is a good reason for practicing it. Rounding over is a healthy stretch for your spine when well done. The weight of your head gives a gentle tractive pull on the whole spine. It's a good way to check that your head is not contracting back and down. And it's a fairly quick way of lengthening your spine if you don't have time to do constructive rest. This would make it a useful exercise to do right before performing, for instance.

- Sit in a chair, *thinking up* through your torso.
- Allow your head to tip down toward your chest.
- Let your torso continue to lengthen.
- Slowly allow your spine to curve over, one vertebra at a time.
- Keep breathing as you slowly curve over, your spine lengthening, until finally you are hanging in between your legs. Your arms hang easily at your sides.
- Exhale three times.
- Count to five. Repeat.
- Slowly uncurve your spine. Use your lower abdominal muscles to support your lower back as you build up your spine one vertebra at a time. The last things to come up are your neck and your head.
- Think of lengthening and widening as you uncurl.
- Repeat the curving over action of the spine, and then building your spine back up again.
- You can also do this exercise standing. Be sure that you bend your knees when you hang forward to take pressure off of your lower back.

Using Spirals to Explore Three-Dimensionality

Sometimes we think of ourselves almost as paper dolls—as a front and a back. We forget we have sides and volume. What may be partly to blame is that we see ourselves in mirrors, usually from the front. Taking yourself through this exercise's movements will help you become more aware of the sides of your body, the volume of it, and its potential range of motion. It feels strong and powerful on the inside and looks that way from the outside, too. It's then useful to maintain this inner sense of expansion even when motionless.

- Stand, being aware of the Alexander concepts.
- Breathe freely.
- Float your arms out to the sides.
- Feel your energy lengthening up along your spine and widening across your shoulders and chest.
- Turn your head first to the right, then allow your body to follow. Turn around to look behind you.
- Don't force the turn. Explore your flexibility without pushing too far.
- Let your head turn to the left, then let your body follow.
- Come through center, and let yourself look behind you.
- These movements give a gentle diagonal stretch through the front and back of your body. You're also finding the three-dimensional quality of your body in the space.
- Do the movement three times on each side. Continue the lengthening along your spine, and the widening through your chest and shoulders.
- Afterward, let your arms float down to your sides.
- Maintain your sense of yourself as a three-dimensional being.

The Marionette

This exercise is a way of isolating the use of the arm without overengaging the shoulders and back. You use the articulation of the joints of the fingers, wrist, elbow, and shoulder in order to move your arm without overstiffening the surrounding parts of your body. It helps your arm to feel light and easy, and can take away a surprising amount of heaviness and tightness that accumulates around the shoulder and upper arm. This tightness often leads to a slumping forward of the shoulder and a retraction of your upper arm into the underarm.

- Recall the Alexander thoughts: *Freeing your neck, letting your head go forward and up, your torso to lengthen and widen.* Think of having smooth, unobstructed breathing.
- Imagine that you are a marionette and someone pulls your strings.

- These strings are attached to the fingers of your right hand. Your fingers stretch up toward the ceiling, bringing the whole arm with it.
- Your arm extends straight up toward the ceiling. Your shoulder stays down.
- You're lengthened and widened.
- Someone tugs on the strings harder, and your fingers stretch further up toward the ceiling, and now your shoulder stretches up, too.
- A string is cut, and you relax your wrist. Your hand hangs down.
- A second string is cut. You relax from the elbow. Your arm hangs down from it. The upper arm is still stretched toward the ceiling.
- The final string is cut. Your whole arm releases down to your side, as though you were a rag doll. Your torso still lengthens up.
- Repeat with the same arm.
- Then tune in. Do your two arms feel different? If so, how? You might feel warmer in the arm you stretched up, or it may feel like it has more "energy" in it.
- Repeat twice with the other arm.
- When you're finished, be aware of the length of your torso, and the freedom, and energetic quality of your arms, resting easily at your sides. They are not stiff or overly lax. And they're not contracted into your underarms; they hang easily from your shoulders.

The Power of Stillness

This is a trust exercise as much as anything else. It's a matter of trusting yourself—that you and your talent are enough. Trusting that just standing there and apparently "doing nothing" will be enough to draw the intent interest of the audience. The power of your thought, emotion, and intention is always there underneath the surface—a palpable force to be reckoned with.

- Find a way of standing that you feel you can maintain for some time.
- Recall the Alexander thoughts: *Let my neck be free, to let my torso lengthen and widen, to let my arms and legs release away from my body.*
- Think wide through your chest and shoulders. Allow your arms to hang freely at your sides.
- Sense your breath moving easily in and out.

- While you will look "still" to the outside observer, know that you are making micromovements in your feet, ankles, and legs. You will be swaying very slightly.
- Check to make sure you're not locking your knees or your lower back.
- Keep your eyes soft, not locked.
- Don't make any large movements. But don't lock and tighten, either.
- Think of your standing as *active*, even though you are "still"—you're not locked and frozen in place.
- See if you can experience the power of stillness comfortably. The power of doing nothing—of just *being*.

6

Breathing

When asked what were the three most important things in acting, Laurence Olivier answered, "Voice, voice, and voice." Obviously, breath is the indispensable prerequisite to this. Every thought, feeling, and impulse initiates from your breath—what Alexander called your *motive-power*. This is an old-fashioned phrase, but a useful one. It implies the initiation and movement of the breath but also the catalyst behind it. In utilizing your motive-power, you will discover your breath in order to speak, sing, move, and act. Free breathing broadens and expands you, offering you more physical and mental space, and opens up myriad personal possibilities. Breathing small tends to lead people into safe acting choices. If you breathe more deeply, more freely, more authentically, it will lead you toward making bold, truthful acting choices. It keeps you focused, confident, and connected to your deeply personal emotional impulses. The breathing exercises below will take you through a personal unfolding process step by step. Working with your breath is one of the most important things you can do in your acting practice. If I were you, I'd commit to working on it every day.

Working on your breathing doesn't necessarily mean you need to "take deep breaths," as people are sometimes advised to do. Too often people overwork and force when they do that. Sucking air in through your nose or mouth actually tightens the throat and restricts your whole breathing mechanism, including your jaw, the root of your tongue, the base of your neck, your shoulders, and your chest. This cuts down on your natural resonance and minimizes your overtones and undertones in speaking and singing. Depending on the individual, it can also add a nasal quality, or a metallic, strained, or muffled quality to the voice. It can often limit both the emotional and musical range of your voice. When you don't use yourself in the easiest way, you don't express yourself fully. You sense this instinctively and you may "work harder" to breathe and "speak well," which often just leads to further tension. It's a negative habit-cycle.

We're looking for the opposite—pure, natural breathing, which babies and animals do instinctively. Breathing is a reflex. It happens without our thinking about it if we "get out of the way." You *can* help nature along if you think about your breathing constructively and intelligently. You can influence it quite a bit, indirectly, through gentle conscious guidance of yourself. Freeing yourself of physical and mental tension will help you liberate your breathing. You can encourage the natural breathing process by allowing things to work more easily so your body and breathing open up over time. Then you will have the breath you need for whatever activity you want to perform: running, dancing, swimming, sports, acting in a play outdoors with no amplification, acting in a film; *standing up and being heard*. Breath is a physical necessity, but it is also an existential statement: "I am here. I exist. I'm alive."

Breath is directly responsible for some of the theater's most exciting moments: Mother Courage's silent scream; George weeping at the grave of Emily in *Our Town*; Blanche's gasp as she sinks to her knees on Stanley's line "We've had this date from the beginning" in *A Streetcar Named Desire*. These are all moments without speech, but in addition to these "silent" moments, every line of dialogue in every play or film requires you not to *take* a breath but to *allow* a breath to come in before you speak. Even if your character stands silently, not saying a word, not reacting to anything, you still breathe. That breath is vital to your character, the scene, and your acting.

I recently watched a scene in a film with three women in it. It takes place on a young woman's wedding day. She's in her wedding gown, in her bedroom, about to go downstairs and get married, and her sophisticated soon-to-be mother-in-law politely explains how she is going to completely dominate her daughter-in-law's life. The young woman touchingly tries to reach out emotionally to her mother-in-law, who is utterly cold. It is a brilliantly written and acted scene, underplayed rather than overstated. I found myself often watching the actor playing the girl's grandmother, who is helpless to aid her granddaughter. She stands silently between the other two women, concerned about the domineering mother-in-law and worried for her granddaughter's future. But she can't say anything because of her lesser social position. You can *see* and *feel* her hold her breath—it's one of the most touching things about the scene. You feel for her. And yet she's giving a silent performance that is largely communicated through her breath. It's important for you to recognize, in whatever you do, just how much will be communicated to the audience through your breath, nonverbally—or perhaps it's more correct to say preverbally, in addition to regular speech.

Every actor receives all kinds of conflicting information about breathing. If you're not careful it can be very confusing. You might hear different things from a director, speech teacher, singing teacher, yoga instructor, or personal trainer. My main point is that you want to *stop doing whatever it is that's holding you back*. The culprit is usually the tightness that is occurring somewhere in the vocal mechanism: the throat, the face and resonators, the intercostal muscles between your ribs, or the musculature around your diaphragm and your back. In fact, tension anywhere in the body can indirectly affect your breathing and the sound of your voice.

Even with all the various opinions on what constitutes "good breathing," there are certain basic fundamentals I think we can all agree on:

- Breath is necessary.
- Tension restricts the breath.
- Freeing the body releases the breath.
- Breathing as simply as a baby or small child, as a place to start, is desirable.
- You want your breath to respond to and feed your every thought and feeling.
- You can be consciously in charge of your breath when you want or need to be.
- Ideally, your breath will be natural and unforced.

Tidal Breathing

Tidal breathing is what your normal breathing is called when you're in a resting state and no extraordinary demands are put on it. It is like the tide of the ocean, flowing in and out. The more you become aware of yourself when you are tidal breathing, the more you'll become aware of habits you may have. Some people tend to tense the upper chest and tighten around the breastbone (sternum). Others tend to tighten and fix the whole rib cage rigidly, so it barely moves. Still others may stiffen the neck and shoulders. The jaw, lips, and tongue can often rigidify as well. Let's work to counteract that tendency. Before you begin this exercise, I recommend going to Jessica Wolf's website, www.artofbreathing.net, to view a three-dimensional video of the breathing process.

- Lie down with a paperback book under your head and your knees bent; or sit quietly.
- Sense-poise-flow. Neck free, head forward and out, torso to lengthen and widen.
- Place your hands on your lower rib cage.

- Sense your breath. How quick or slow is it?
- Is it even or uneven?
- Do you sense one side of your rib cage moving more than the other?
- Does your upper chest move more than your lower rib cage? Or does the rib cage not move at all?
- Are you aware of anything in your neck and shoulders when you breathe? Your back? Place your hands there to sense what is happening.
- Are you able to leave your eyes open while you focus on your breathing?
- Are you able to be aware of your environment and your breathing at the same time?
- Are you able to sense the flow of the air in and out?

Rib Cage Movement

For whatever reason, many people tend to tighten their rib cages. Even dogs and cats do this when they get frightened. It's good to remember that although the rib cage is strong and is there to protect your heart, lungs, spinal cord, and other vital organs, ideally it should be in constant motion, moving in and out with your breathing. An elastic, moving object is stronger than a static, rigid one. The motion in and out is part of what draws your breath into your lungs, along with the up-and-down motion of the diaphragm. If you allow your ribs to swing in and out freely, it helps to calm your breathing, your nervous system, and your emotions. It's best to do this exercise with a partner, though you can do it on your own.

- Stand behind your partner and gently place your hands around her lower rib cage.
- Stay easy within yourself as your partner breathes.
- What do you notice?
- Does your partner's rib cage move at all?
- Does part of it move more than another part?
- Does the movement seem smooth or jerky? Is it integrated or cut off from the rest of her body?
- What do you notice about the rate of speed and depth of her breathing?
- Don't be prescriptive for your partner or tell her how to change. Be open-minded and nonjudgmental about what you sense.

- Have your partner count to five out loud a few times. What do you sense in her body as she counts? Then have her count to ten several times. What do you notice?
- Change places. Have your partner go through the same process with you.

Blowing Out the Candle

This is a very calming breath exercise. Since it is so elementary, it doesn't seem like it does much—which is true. It *undoes*; it unlocks what's holding you back. Each time you practice, it helps your mind-body let go a little bit more. As you breathe, you might imagine peeling layers off an onion. You get closer and closer to the core, less defended, and more connected to your "center." If you have patience, it will help give you the opposite of immediate results. It will help you build a peaceful and steady drumbeat—the in-and-out motion of tidal breathing—that works in tandem with your heartbeat.

- Lie down with a paperback book under your head and your knees bent. Place your hands on your lower rib cage.
- Think through the Alexander thoughts: Let your neck be free, your head to release forward and out, your torso to lengthen and widen.
- Allow your breath to flow in and out easily.
- Sense your breath underneath your hands. See you if you can feel it moving inside your body, without "making it happen."
- Allow an easy breath to fall in through your nose—don't force it.
- Gently purse your lips and blow out through your mouth, as though you are blowing out a candle in slow motion. A slow, controlled breath.
- Do that two more times.
- Rest for several moments.
- Blow out three more times. Rest for several moments. Then blow out three more times. Do three sets of three breaths each.

The Whispered "Ah"

Like blowing out the candle, the whispered "ah" is a simple exercise. Its simplicity is part of its elegance and effectiveness. Much of the power is in what you *don't* do. It helps you breathe more easily, more deeply, more freely, seemingly without any effort. It brings you more in touch with your mind-body, your emotions, and the connection between them. I personally practice this exercise every day. It's an excellent way to keep yourself calm and gently focused.

- Lie down with your knees bent. Your head rests on a paperback book to keep your head from retracting back and down.
- Place your hands on your lower rib cage.
- Sense your body against the floor, your head against the paperback book.
- Allow your body to release and fall back into the floor.
- Let your body gently lengthen and widen. This happens through your thought and intention.
- Let your neck be free, to let your head release forward and out, to let your torso lengthen and widen. Let your arms and legs release away from your body, and your chest and shoulders to be open.
- Think of a small, internal smile, like that of Mona Lisa. This gently activates the muscles of your face and your eyes.
- Allow your breath to drop gently in through your nose.
- Whisper out on an extended "ah." It's like you're saying the word "ah" but whispering it.
- It's a long, slow, controlled exhale. Don't force the air and don't try to extend the breath longer than is comfortable.
- Make certain your body isn't collapsing as you breathe out. Leave your body free, especially the neck, head, shoulders, and back.
- Do two more whispered "ah"s. Then pause for several moments so you don't "overbreathe."
- Remember your subtle, internal smile as you do three more whispered "ah"s.
- This helps to release the soft palate up in the back. You don't have to make it happen. It's organic when you think of a small smile.
- Pause for several seconds.
- Do a final set of three whispered "ah"s, with an internal smile, which helps gently energize the whole face.

Resonance

Most resonance happens in your face, head, neck, chest, and rib cage, but your whole body is a resonating chamber; vibrations happen throughout your entire body. The more released you are, the more resonant you will be. Resonance is part of what conveys emotion when you speak or sing. Any tension deadens your musculature, muffles your sound, and cuts down on the undertones and overtones in your voice as well as your expression. You may also do this exercise with a partner to sense the vibrations in each other.

- Lie on the floor, a paperback book under your head. Arms resting on your lower ribs.
- Have your legs straight out on the ground. Place pillows or rolled-up towels under your knees to keep your lower back from overarching.
- Allow your body to release into the floor. Sense the support from the ground.
- Think through your Alexander thoughts, to release and coordinate yourself.
- Let your neck be free, to let your head release forward and out, to let your torso lengthen and widen.
- Do three blowing out the candles.
- Do three whispered "ah"s. These will help release your breath and free your mind-body even more.
- Hum somewhere near the middle of your vocal range.
- Be aware of the buzzing on your lips.
- Sense the buzzing and the resonance in your face: your forehead, temples, cheeks, nose, and jaw. If you like, use your hands to feel it.
- Feel the buzzing in your neck: in the front, back, and sides.
- Use your hands to be aware of the vibrations in your shoulders and chest.
- Move your hands farther down, to your middle and lower rib cage.
- Place your hands under your lower back to sense the vibrations there.
- See if you can sense small vibrations in your arms and legs.
- Be aware of the resonance in your whole body: head, neck, torso, legs, and arms.
- If you find it challenging to be aware of your whole body at the same time, then allow your consciousness to sweep from your head through your feet, then back to your head again—almost like a lighthouse shining its light in a circle.
- Stop humming. See if you can be aware of the remnants of the reverberation, even after you stop humming.

Whispered "Ah" and Counting

This exercise will help your body become used to easy, free-flowing breathing in the upright position. The whispered "ah" helps get things going, and then you gently bring yourself into simple speech. The moment when you begin to count is a critical point when your old habits of tightening may want to come back in. If you feel yourself tensing in that moment—not to worry. Return to the process of leaving yourself as free as possible as you breathe, and gently transition into counting again.

- Think your flow suggestions: Let your neck be free, to let your head go forward and up.
- Place your hands on your lower rib cage. Keep your fingers and palms easy.
- Observe your own breathing.
- Sense if there is any movement in your ribs. Have the intention of the intercostal muscles (between your ribs) being easy.
- Do three whispered "ah"s.
- See if you can allow your lower ribs to gently move together on your exhales.
- The ribs will open slightly as you inhale. Don't suck air in on the inhale, and don't force your ribs to open or close. The movement may be subtle at first; it will gradually increase over time.
- Do three more whispered "ah"s. Think an internal smile. Allow your ribs to be as flexible as possible.
- It's almost like when you're standing in a pool up to your chest. There is a buoyancy, and flowing movement as you breathe. As though you are supported by the water.
- Count to five out loud, continuing to allow a gentle movement of the ribs.
- Repeat a few times. Count to ten a few times out loud.

"Filling Yourself with Helium"

This exercise gives you a chance to encourage a lightness and smoothness in your body, as did the exercise when you imagined yourself as a hollow flute (page xxx).

- Bring yourself into constructive rest.
- Center your breathing and your mind.
- Think through your poise-flow thoughts. Say a gentle "no" to your tension habits, and "yes" to your Alexander directions.
- Imagine that your body is hollow.
- Work your way from the top of your body to the bottom. Thinking, "Hollow head, hollow neck, hollow shoulders, hollow torso, hollow arms, hollow legs. My whole body is hollow."

- Slowly imagine your body filling with helium. Your head, neck, shoulders, torso, arms, legs—your whole body.
- Imagine the helium moving around inside your whole body. Filling it with a light energy.
- Move your arms, one at a time, then together, to see what it feels like to be full of helium.
- Move one leg at a time: thinking of being full of helium.
- Move your head slowly back and forth on the book. Nod up and down (head still on the book). Think of being full of helium.
- Move any body part you like in this way.
- Slowly imagine the helium escaping slowly from your body.
- Gradually you return to your "regular body." You will feel lighter, airier.
- Stand, and take a moment to gather yourself. Then walk.
- What's it like to walk with this much lightness and lack of downward pressure?

Organic Expression

7

Using Your Imagination

In the first part of the book, we discussed the Alexander principles—awareness, poise, and flow—and ways of integrating them into your everyday life and your work in the performing arts. In this section of the book, I've laid out a number of exercises I designed to stimulate and develop your imagination and emotions. All these specially designed procedures are based on the Alexander principles, so you're never meant to push or force anything. The exercises are crafted to help you learn more about yourself and to open you up, in all your aspects, in an effortless manner. They will help you to release by letting go of tension and old unconstructive mind-body habits, connecting to your breath, your true voice, and your innate talent. Then you take all of that and apply it to *movement*.

The main things to remember are that you are building awareness, pausing and poising when you come up against old habits, saying a "positive no" to them, and giving yourself the directions to help guide you in your new way of being.

Opening Your Mind-Body

This is a peaceful way to work through your whole body. You can take your time. It's almost as if you are oiling each part and putting them all together to work as a harmonious whole. It can be used effectively at any time, but is especially helpful before and after rehearsals, auditions, and performances. Use your imagination to see each body part in your mind's eye. And see each part as part of your whole body.

- Bring yourself into constructive rest position.
- Use any of the breathing techniques we've discussed to help you release.
- Think through your Alexander suggestions.
- Gently turn your head, in slow motion, from side to side, as if you're saying no.
- Leave your head against the book as you do this. Don't lift it up off the book, as that will produce strain.
- Bring your head back to the center.
- Leaving your head on the book, gently nod your head up and down, as if you're saying yes.
- It's a small, subtle movement. Think of moving from the top of the spine, which is between your ears, behind your nose. Quite high up.
- Bring yourself back to center.
- Put the two small movements together: nod your head up and down and slowly turn your head from side to side at the same time.
- These gentle movements help you to release your neck.
- Think through your coordinating ideas again: *Neck free, head balanced, torso long and wide. Arms and legs to release away from your body.*
- Drape your arms across your body, as if you are hugging yourself. This helps you release in between your shoulder blades in the back. Remain here for a bit.
- Spread your arms out to either side, along the floor. This helps to open your chest and shoulders. It's not an active stretch, it's passive. The position *is* the stretch. Allow your arms and shoulders to fall back toward the floor.
- Bring your hands back to rest on your lower rib cage.
- Think through your Alexander suggestions. Your body will progressively get freer and freer.
- Gently bring one knee up toward your chest. Place your hands on your knee to support it. How close you bring your knee in doesn't matter. You are very gently releasing your lower back.
- Bring that leg back down, bend your other knee up toward your chest, and support it with your hands.
- If it's comfortable for you, bring both knees up toward your chest, with a hand on each knee, to support the gentle release through your lower back.
- Gently make very small circles with your hands, to guide your knees in small circular movements. This will rock your lower back a bit, easing it.
- Come back to a central position. A hand on each knee.
- With your hands, slowly and easily move your knees a few inches to the right, then back through center, and then a few inches to the left. Easily move the knees from side to side several times. This will help ease your lower back.
- Bring yourself back to neutral: bent knees, feet on the floor.

- Remind yourself of your Alexander thoughts. Give two whispered "ah"s.
- If you are comfortable with the movement, stretch your arms above your head, lying on the floor. Think of length along your spine and through your arms.
- Return to center.
- Easily turn your head from side to side.
- Return to center. Think through your Alexander suggestions.
- Allow yourself to breathe easily.
- Whisper "ah" three times.
- Have a sense of how you have changed after the exercise.

The Cosmic X

This is a way to give yourself the visceral experience of expanding out in all directions. Working with this exercise a number of times will help you to actualize this concept in your everyday movement. When you bring this image with you into an audition, it will automatically bring charisma into the room with you.

- Take yourself through some of the previous exercises, so that your body is released and open.
- Bring yourself into constructive rest, with your head on a book and your knees bent.
- Think through your Alexander thoughts. Allow your breathing to be free.
- Think length through one of your legs as you allow it straighten along the floor.
- Think length through your other leg as you straighten it. Both are now straightened on the floor.
- Stay easy in your neck, shoulders, and lower back.
- Spread your arms open above your head, in a large V.
- Open your legs into a V.
- Your body is now in a large X shape.
- Imagine having a long spine with your head balanced at the top.
- Imagine being tall through your arms and legs.
- Imagine yourself as a cosmic X stretching out in five directions (your head and spine and each of your limbs) into infinity.
- Breathe easily. Give three whispered "ah"s.
- Remind yourself that your body stretches out in five directions into infinity.

- Bring yourself back into constructive rest. Knees bent.
- Stay here for a while. Do three more whispered "ah"s.
- Stand and walk, staying with the idea of the flow of energy going in five directions.
- Try working with the concept as you walk down the street, and see how you feel.

Color and Energy

I've never come across anyone who doesn't enjoy this fun exercise. You get so focused on the energy and the color that you aren't very aware of the movement at first. People perform this exercise with a released concentration, so their movement is freed up. Do this exercise with a partner or in a group.

- Face your partner. If in a group, stand in a circle.
- Put your hands quite close together. Get a sense of the energy between your two hands. Some people can feel it a bit more easily if their eyes are closed for a few moments.
- Move your hands a little bit apart. You are "stretching" the energy.
- Move your hands together and apart several times. You're able to change the shape of the energy at will.
- Gradually take your hands farther and farther apart, seeing if you can maintain the sense of the energy between your hands. If you ever feel you lose contact with it, bring your hands close together again until your reestablish the contact.
- Take whatever shapes and movements you feel like.
- Choose a color. In your mind's eye, make the energy between your hands that color. Continue to move the colorful energy between your hands.
- Pass your energy balls back and forth with your partner or the group.
- If you like, you can try and guess what the colors are.
- Let the colors gets more intense and saturated in your mind.
- If want to try, see if you can throw the balls of energy back and forth.
- Take one of the balls of energy above your head, and bring it down over your body. Imagine that your whole body is the energy of that color.
- Walk around the room. Imagine that as you walk, you are leaving footprints of that color. When you move your hands and arms, you leave streaks of color through the air. The top of your head leaves streaks of color on the ceiling.

- Gather the energy from your body back into a small ball.
- Gradually make the ball smaller and smaller, so that you can easily move and stretch it between your hands.
- At last, take the ball and gently throw it up into to the air, and let it float away.
- Try walking down the street imagining the color inside you.

Circles of Attention

These are some of my variations on the classic Stanislavski concept of circles of attention. There are a number of ways to work with them; my approach is to keep the exercise simple and direct so that you can have a clear connection to it. There will be many times this exercise can be usefully applied to stage work, especially with regard to the famous *fourth wall*, the imaginary wall between you and the audience. But it's also extremely useful for use in film when discriminating between long shots, medium shots, and close-ups.

- Sit at a desk or a table. Think through your Alexander directions.
- Imagine you are sitting on a dark stage.
- There is pin-spot lighting only your hands and wrists.
- Watch your own hands type on a computer or handheld device. Or write on a piece of paper.
- Allow your focus to be only on your hands and what you are writing.
- Don't "block out" the rest of what's around you, just don't give your attention to it.
- How does it feel in your body, your breathing, your mind-emotions as you do this?
- Now imagine the light is a spotlight that is illuminating your arms from the elbows down to your hands. Also, the desk or table is illuminated.
- Give your focus to your lower arms, hands, and the surface you are working on.
- Observe your own movements. Take note of the sound of your typing, or writing. Be aware of your own rhythm.
- Check in with your body-breath-mind-emotions.
- Now imagine that the spotlight is larger. Your whole body is lit, as well as the area two feet around you in all directions, including above your head.
- Have a sense of that space around you, as well as your entire self.
- The next spotlight illuminates half the room.

- Continue your typing or writing. Be aware of that space, and what is happening within that space visually and aurally, as well as within yourself, as a totality.
- Monitor your breathing, your movements, your self. See if you can guide your emotions and thoughts to the activity you're engaged in.
- The next spotlight fills the entire room. Don't consciously make yourself do anything different because of this. See if your awareness of yourself in the environment changes anything within you.
- Note your breathing, how you're sitting and typing, what's happening with your thoughts and feelings.
- Bring yourself back to the smallest spot—the pin spot.
- Your focus is more concentrated on a small area now, your hands, and what you're writing.
- Take note of how that feels different than the largest circle.
- In your own time, change your focus of attention at will. From one size circle to another. At whatever tempo you choose.
- Give your attention to yourself as you do this.
- Try walking in different-size circles of attention. Walk in a small circle, giving your attention only to that space. Then a slightly larger circle, a medium-size circle, a large circle, and then finally walking the whole room.
- What does it feel like to you as your circle of attention gets larger?
- How is your movement affected? Your mind-emotions?
- Try the exercise again, using any movements you like: large or small. Use your creativity. Try going back and forth between the different circles.
- Imagine the circles of attention on different kinds of stages: proscenium, thrust, and in the round. Imagine yourself moving across the stage in whatever way you choose. What's it like to have the audience on different sides? Does that affect your circles of attention? How?

Magic Carpet

I call this the magic carpet exercise because it's almost like magic when you can change your state of being and your movement just by thinking about them. It's very useful to feel its effects on your partner, and you'll sense how clearly her intention changes her entire mind-body. Try it when you're working on the *magic if*. "What would happen if I were this kind of person, living in that time, in that place?" You're using your mind to affect how you feel and how you behave.

- Stand easily.
- Think through your Alexander thoughts.
- Ask yourself to become *heavy*. That is your intention.
- Your body will follow your thought. It will follow through without you forcing it. Trust that.
- Raise your arm. The movement will be heavy, because you asked your body to be heavy.
- Raise your other arm. That will be heavy as well.
- Wave. Have a sense of how an easy movement can be difficult, if it's dead weight.
- Let your arms flop down heavily.
- Turn your head. Shrug your shoulders. Move your hips. You'll do this heavily, because it's your intention. Have a sense of how your mind affects your body.
- Walk around the room. Your movement will be affected by your thought process. Sense what your heavy walk is like.
- Now change your intention. Make your whole self *light* through your thought.
- If images help you, use them. You can imagine you are full of air or helium.
- Move your arms, your legs, hands, and feet.
- Walk, skip, hop if you like.
- What is it like to do that? What is it like to *be* light?
- Change your intention again. To be *jagged*.
- Try various movements, staying with your intention to be jagged. Walk in this manner. Try any movement in a jagged manner.
- Change your intention to *smooth*.
- Try a series of movements in a smooth way. Sense how smooth is the opposite of jagged. And different than heavy and light.
- If you're able to do the exercise with a partner, she can move your arm to see what that feels like when your arms is heavy. Then she can go through the intentions light, smooth, and jagged. She can test moving your head and your shoulders. She can take note of the differences.
- Go back and forth between the contrasting states of *freeze* and *flow*. When working with the freezing state, take yourself through walking and other simple movements, and purposefully sometimes freezing and holding.
- When you are working with the contrasting state of flow, allow all your movements to go smoothly from one to the next, in an easy manner.

Given Circumstances

Given circumstances are everything. What happens in your mind-body with each of the scenarios? The action is the same, but *how* you do it is vastly different. What you're thinking and especially what you're feeling will dictate your movement.

- Think sense-poise-flow. You are aware, inhibit your unconstructive habits, and give yourself the Alexander directions.
- Breathe low and slow.
- Choose a simple action, such as open a door, come into the room, and close the door.
- Do it with the following *given circumstances*:
  a. You're coming home from work. You're exhausted and depressed.
  b. You're late. Your date is going to be here in five minutes. You have to clean the whole room before he gets here.
  c. A childhood friend you haven't seen in ten years is coming to dinner.
  d. A crazy man chased you down the street. You barely get inside and close the door behind you to keep him from getting in.
  e. The front door was unlocked and you know you locked it when you left. You think there may be an intruder in your apartment.

Anatomy

Becoming familiar with the way your body works best will help you prevent injuries as well as avoid tightness and stress. Keeping the machine that is yourself in good working order will pay long-term benefits.

- Go online to http://www.nlm.nih.gov/exhibition/historicalanatomies/vesalius_home.html
- Take a few minutes to look at the structure of the body. Both the bones and the muscles. The bones give us our structure. The muscles help us locomote. The brain gives us instructions, and the nervous system conducts the messages from the brain to the muscles. Imagine how that affects the way we move.
- Looking at the illustrations, see how the head is poised at the top of the spine.

- Note how the head is balanced above the shoulder girdle.
- Notice the length of the spine from the top, at about the level of the ears, all the way to down the *coccyx* (tailbone).
- Observe the natural curves of the spine: a natural forward curve through the neck, a backward curve through the upper back, a forward curve through the low back, and a backward curve through the *sacral* area, near the bottom of the spine.
- Notice how the arms attach to the torso.
- See how the legs fit into the hip joints.
- Take a look at how the hands and feet are structured.
- Imagine how this elegant structure moves through space.
- Imagine this structure walking, standing, sitting, bending, reaching, jumping, running, lifting weights, and doing yoga or pilates.
- Visualize this structure singing and dancing.
- Find an illustration you want to work on and take on that pose. Put yourself in the same position as the illustration.
- Stay there, and see what you need to do to be comfortable in that position.
- Find different poses and take those on.
- Walk around your home, and do different activities, imagining your structure underneath your skin: the bones and muscles. See the structure doing the activities in your mind's eye.

Tracing the Spine

- Observe the movement of a dog, cat, or horse. It's easy to see how the head leads and the body follows. It's the same in human beings, though we're a little different from our four-legged friends. Your head going forward and up helps to lengthen your spine. Then your legs move you forward in space. Do this exercise with a partner.
- Stand behind your partner. Place a finger on either side of her spine, just below her neck.
- Trace your partner's spine. Take your time. Sense the shape of the spine. Travel down her neck, through the upper back, middle back, lower back, to the tailbone.
- Then travel back up again with two fingers.

- See if you can gain a sense that the spine is a central organizing system for the body.
- Have your partner trace your spine.
- What is it like to sense each of your own vertebrae as they are being traced? We don't often take the time to think about this important part of the body.
- Walk around the room with your partner's hands touching your spine.
- Stay aware of what your spine is doing as you move.
- From a sitting position, roll all the way forward, until your head is hanging in between your legs. Your partner's hands remain on your spine. This will help you have a sense of what your spine is doing in this movement.
- Be aware of what your spine is doing as you roll up, using your stomach muscles to support your back.
- Do side stretches in both directions, with your partner's hands on your spine to help to heighten your awareness.
- Now you do the same for your partner on these three movements.

The Psychological Gesture

This is my interpretation of a classic exercise that was created by the acting teacher Michael Chekhov. Even if the exercise feels slightly awkward at first, try to stay with it. It can feel pretty "theatrical" to some actors. But if you commit to it, and perform it authentically, it can be very helpful, almost primal in its effectiveness.

- Choose a specific character that you are working on.
- Visualize that character: whatever you know or are exploring about her.
- Look through visual images that inspire you for this character. You can look at magazines and online.
- The images can be of people and animals, or they can be abstract.
- What aspects of these images attract you?
- What aspects of these images relates to the character you're working on?
- Who is your character? What are her wants?
- Where does she live? Work? What is her relation to the other characters? The story?

- How is your mind-body similar to hers'? Are there things about her that you relate to, even if she is a villain, for instance?
- How do you visualize her body? Her clothing? Her movement?
- How do you see her walking, sitting, standing, and so on? Why does she move that way?
- What would you say the general "energy" of her movement is?
- How might other people react to her, and her body language? Does she tend to attract, allure, or repel people? Or all of the above?
- Stand up and begin to explore how she might move based on all this. If something doesn't feel right, it doesn't matter—try something else.
- When you find a movement or a gesture that works, repeat it a few times until it feels organic to you.
- If it helps you, listen to music as you move—anything that stimulates your imagination.
- Try different speeds for her movements. Different intentions. Even if it's "wrong," you'll learn something about her.
- How might she speak? Read something out loud as she might.
- Explore what might be similar to your voice, and what might be different. What part of the world did she come from? When was she born? How many people were in her family? Did she need to fight to be heard?
- Visualize a single gesture that "embodies" her. It can be subtle, large, or even exaggerated. Whatever gesture encapsulates her for you.
- Do the gesture. If it doesn't ring true to you, try it again, or try a different gesture.
- Experiment until you find something that sums up all that she is to you.
- You can repeat this at will when working on the role. It will help bring you immediately into the center of the character.

Music

We all know how powerful music can be. This exercise helps bring you out of your head and into your body. Some of my suggestions will be surprisingly challenging, especially when I ask you to make movements that are in opposition to the music. The objective is certainly not to do the exercise "perfectly" or even "well" but to find freedom within yourself. You may find it helpful to hear music in your mind before you enter a scene if it promotes an emotional state or intensity in yourself that is beneficial for the scene.

- Using music from *The Rite of Spring* by Stravinsky:
  - Stomp in time to the music.
  - Stomp deliberately out of time to the music.
  - Crawl on your belly, using your hands and legs.
  - Crawl on your belly, using just your legs to move you forward.
  - Walk around the room sideways.
  - Choreograph a two-minute dance to the music, using sharp, staccato movements.
- Using music from *Swan Lake* by Tchaikovsky:
  - Take objects off a shelf in time to the music.
  - Pick up sheets of paper off the floor in time to the music.
  - Walk with one foot directly in front of the other.
  - Walk backwards, in rhythm, but in half time.
  - Stand still and move just your arms in time to the music.
  - Wash the dishes, having your body move to the music in whatever way you like.
- Using music from the latest dance hit:
  - Stand still without moving.
  - Skip rope to the music. (Or pretend to skip rope if you don't have one.)
  - Type on the computer, allowing your body to move to the music as you type.
  - Try singing a different song as this music plays.
  - Let yourself dance to the music as though you were in a club.
  - Let yourself march, but deliberately off the beat.

Tempo-Rhythms

Although you may have much in common with some of the characters you play, you may also have a different tempo or rhythm from theirs, so they may appear to the audience as somewhat different from you. Stanislavksi calls rhythm an inner level of intensity that manifests itself outwardly. This is one way that you can explore that territory.

- Walk in your usual manner.
- Take note of what you do as you walk.
- Now walk quickly. See what that is like.
- Walk slowly. Be aware of how your body adjusts to the movement.
- Now walk at a medium speed. See how your body reacts to your instruction.
- Switch back and forth between the three speeds at will.
- Walk at the three speeds again, but this time find a motivation for each of the speeds. For instance, you can walk quickly because you are late for an audition.
- Find a motivation for walking at a medium tempo. For instance, you might be called as a witness in a trial, and you are walking into the courtroom.
- Find a reason for walking slowly. You could be going to a church to attend a memorial service.
- Do the exercise with a partner. Perform the walks together but choose contrasting tempo-rhythms. Make sure not to pick up on your partner's choice.
- Try the exercise a few more times. One of you be the leader. Again choose a contrasting tempo-rhythm on purpose, but then allow yourself to be influenced by your partner's choice. Come into her tempo-rhythm.
- Switch roles so that you are the leader and your partner will be influenced by you.

Using Different Centers of the Body

Try this exercise with a partner or in a group. It helps to have feedback on what you're doing and to see how other people transform during the exercise. If you do it on your own, you can use a camera to record yourself. Though it may seem like primarily an "external" exercise, your choices will often naturally provoke surprisingly strong emotional reactions.

- Choose a "center" for your body—the chest, for example. Let that part of your body be primary in your mind, and let it lead your movement. So, in walking, the chest might move forward first.
- Try walking, sitting, standing, running, picking something up off the floor, reading out loud, and so on. See how this center affects your movement. Allow yourself to be bold in your choices.
- Perform the actions again. This time keep things quite subtle. Keep it something that's happening on the inside, that you know about, but might not show much on the outside.

- See how this intention affects you.
- Hear from your partner(s) what they saw, or watch the video you took of yourself.
- If working with others, reverse roles.
- Perform the exercise several times, using several different parts of yourself as your center: your chest, your neck, your right shoulder, and so on.
- Take note of how you behave differently with the different centers.
- Also note how it affects you when you deliberately keep the centers noticeable and when you keep them more internal and subtle.
- Try applying the idea of "emotional center" to various parts of the body. Meaning, choose a body part that seems to house most of your emotions.
- Where do you choose? What does it feel like to house most of your emotions in one central place in your body?

Greek Tragedy or Comedy

It feels good to work in styles other than contemporary realism. It stretches your instrument on every level. You can take what you learn and apply it to your naturalistic work.

- Choose a Greek tragedy or comedy for the exercise.
- Choose the character you want to work on.
- Familiarize yourself with the character, the scene, and the situation she is in.
- If you are doing a scene from a tragedy, go online and look at photographs of people in disasters. You'll see people's faces and bodies in extreme poses of tragedy and loss. Memorize some of the positions and use them in the scene.
- If you are doing a scene from a comedy, look for photos of real people in the same extreme situation your character is in. Study the positions the people are in and memorize them.
- Play the scene. Throw yourself full-force into the situations. Greek comedies and tragedies are intense. Use the research you did online.
- Even though you may shout or execute vigorous physical actions, stay as free as possible in your voice and body. That will help you "go all the way" in the scene.

Expensive Clothes

This exercise is a homage to a friend of mine. I first developed it for her. I wanted her to work on a character who was extremely privileged. And I wanted her to have the visceral sensation of what it was like to have very fine clothing on her body and to imagine what it would be like to have that at all times. To imagine that the whole life of her character was like that: the best homes, cars, vacations, and so on. She loved the exercise, and brought a close friend with her; they had a great time. The exercise works just as well for men.

- Put on your most expensive clothing.
- Go to your town's most exclusive store. Bring a friend, if you like.
- Go to the priciest department to shop for a dress or a suit.
- Choose clothing that you would never consider buying because it is so expensive, but you really like.
- Take it to the dressing room and try it on.
- What does it feel like to wear clothing you really like, made out of such great fabric, with an expert cut?
- How do you feel when you look at yourself in the mirror?
- What's it like to walk, sit, and move in the clothes?
- Imagine that you could buy clothing like this anytime you like. Imagine you could buy anything in the store. Imagine you could buy the whole store.
- Try on other items, if you like. Luxurious sweaters, trousers, skirts.
- Return all the items.
- Go to other exclusive stores and repeat. Give yourself the whole afternoon if possible. And you might as well have a drink or a coffee at a nice place afterward, as long as you are in your best clothes.

Multiple Characters

This exercise is designed to be ridiculous. Rather than being afraid of making a mistake or an unfortunate acting choice, embrace the absurdity. If you do the exercise with a partner, attempt to outdo each other. The exercise helps make you brave. It also encourages you to take risks, even to the point of crashing and burning. It's worth it, and you just may find something surprisingly fresh and useful in all your explorations.

- Choose a monologue or a piece of text.
- Do the monologue in several different ways, at different speeds, in different moods, in different accents, and as different ages.
- Try the monologue as a corrupt politician.
- A bad opera singer.
- A clown in a circus.
- A truck driver.
- A cowboy.
- A stand-up comedian.
- Any other character you can think of.
- Switch back and forth from one character to another. Change on a dime.

8

Conscious Imitation of Others

In the last chapter we looked at one of your most powerful tools as an actor: your imagination, and how to access it to help generate your creativity in crafting arresting performances on stage and screen. Forming a clear and specific image, both in your mind and body, is an ingenious way of bringing your conceptions into the real world—into a play or film. What starts as your fantasy (a fancy synonym for the more childlike word "make-believe") takes shape first in your mind, and then through your muscles, bones, breath, voice, emotions, and hard work, you actually bring it "into the room." This is the creative process.

In this section of the book, we're looking at all kinds of ways of working with your breath, voice, body, movement, thoughts, and emotions and helping to blend all these components together to encourage you to be a spontaneous, integrated whole: an actor. In this chapter we'll cover the essential technique of observation and imitation of others. It's a must. For your behavior in a play or film to ring true, you need to be an expert observer, and almost an amateur psychologist, to understand why people feel what they feel and do what they do—and to replicate that behavior in your performances.

Observing Others

It's always easier to notice the mental and physical habits of others than it is to notice your own. But through watching other people and their habits, you'll become better at observing your own. Give special attention to how people balance their heads on the end of their spines. See if you can notice when people tighten their necks and compress their heads down onto their necks and torsos. See if it's possible for you to imitate some of the naturalness ease of children and animals—that's what you're looking for in your own performances.

- Sit down in a busy place—perhaps a mall or a bustling corner during rush hour or lunch hour.
- Observe people as they walk by. What are they doing with their bodies? Do they lean forward or back as they walk? Do you see necks craning forward? Arched lower backs? How do the arms swing? Is the walk even? How are people carrying things? Can you guess where they're going? Or who they might be?
- Watch television with the sound muted and observe the actors' body language. What do people do with their heads, necks, and shoulders? What do you notice about how people use their bodies? What do they do with themselves when they speak and gesticulate?
- Watch talk shows to see how the interviewers and interviewees use themselves. Do they lean in or away from each other? How are they gesturing? Do they seem comfortable in their bodies? What happens in their faces as they communicate?
- Go to the zoo and observe the animals. Can you see the head leading the whole body when they move? What adjectives would you use to describe the animals' movement? Smooth, jerky, or unexpected? How does the animal move when it is emotional? What animal would you like to imitate? What can you learn from the animals' movement that you could apply to your own?
- Watch small children on the street or at the mall. Especially when children are six years of age or younger, they have naturally graceful and flowing movements. Note how they balance their heads and move their bodies as a total unit. Watch the spontaneity and lack of tension. Can you remember being that age? What did your movement feel like at that time?

Observation of Other People's Breathing

As you hone your observational skills, you'll learn to discern subtleties in movement, body language, breathing, and speech. You may find that you have similar habits to some people you observe.

- Observe news anchors on television.
- How do they use their bodies, generally, as they speak?
- How do they handle reading from papers or from monitors?
- Do you have a sense of what's happening with their breathing?
- Do you notice any tension in the face, jaw, forehead, or neck? What about the shoulders and torso?

- If you do notice tension, how do you think it affects the sound of their voices?
- Watch videos online of actors, singers, and politicians.
- What sense do you get of them overall as they speak and move? How do they use themselves?
- What do you notice about their breathing?
- How is it connected to what is happening in their bodies, especially the head, neck, shoulders, and torso?
- How does this affect the sounds of their voices, their tone, and their speech patterns?
- Make notes in your mind-body journal.
- How does this observation relate to your own breathing?

Observation of Great Use

This exercise can be great fun as well as educational. Spend a little time finding the people whom you relate to, whether they are actors, singers, dancers, or athletes. Give yourself the luxury of watching them in several different videos and allow their movements and ways of being to permeate you. Some of what you learn will be conscious and some will be subconscious. Analyze whatever you can. Imitate what you find helpful. Adapt it to your own body, even though your body is different from that of the person you are studying. Imagine what it's like to move as they do and feel as they do, not only when they are engaged in the activities that you are observing but also in their everyday lives.

- Find videos of performers or athletes you admire.
- Watch videos of the person you choose.
- Take note of that person's movement. What is your overall sense of how he or she moves? What are the adjectives you would use to describe the movement?
- How is the relationship between that person's head and neck? How would you describe the poise you see?
- How does the person's head poise relate to the rest of the body and its movement?
- Choose a section of the video to watch several times. See if you can see how your chosen person accomplishes one particular movement—not just what the body parts are doing but what the body as a totality is doing.

- Take a simple section of the movement that you would like to imitate. It could be as simple as lifting an arm. Lift your arm as you do normally. Now see if you can mirror what the person is doing in the video.
- Add the Alexander component. What happens if you *let your neck be free, your torso lengthen and widen*, and your breath stay easy as you explore the movement?

Imitating Someone on the Street

This is a very effective way to give you a sense of other people—who they are, how they are feeling, and where they are going—in reality and in fantasy. It's also an excellent way of complementing all the emotional work you do on a character.

- Choose a time when you're not in a hurry and can focus on the exercise.
- Spot someone on the street who catches your eye in some way.
- Follow him at some distance, so he isn't aware of being observed.
- Observe him. Get a sense of him overall.
- Then begin to analyze his use of himself.
- Note the relationship of his head to his neck and to his torso as he walks. Is his head squashed down onto his neck, or is it poised, with the spine naturally lengthened?
- Do his arms and legs swing easily?
- What about his hips? Do they move easily, or are they locked in place?
- Does he walk flat-footed, or with his toes turned in?
- What kind of bag does he carry, and how heavy do you think it is?
- Can you get a feeling of his overall emotional state from his movement, from how he is walking? What would you say that is?
- Begin to "take on" his walk.
- See if you can get "in sync" with him. Pick up his energy as well as his movement.
- Can you mirror his emotional state as well?
- Where do you think he is walking, and how does that influence his movement?
- How does it feel "being him"?

Imitating Your Colleagues

Imitating a colleague is different from imitating a stranger on the street. You'll have more conscious and unconscious knowledge about your colleague, and it's something you're doing together, in tandem. It's fascinating how movement changes the way you feel. *Imitating physical actions will give you a specific emotional reaction.* Watching colleagues imitate you might make you a little self-conscious, but it's certainly enlightening. There are so many things we do that we're not aware of.

- Do this exercise in a group.
- Stand in a circle.
- One of you is "it" and comes into the center of the circle.
- The person who is "it" walks as she does habitually, without thinking about it.
- Observe closely how she moves.
- How is her head balanced at the top of her spine? Is her head pulled back and down onto her neck? Or pulling to one side? Is her neck jutting forward?
- Is she slumped over? Or does she walk in military fashion? Does she look fairly upright, but still stiff, or somewhat awkward?
- Do her arms swing easily? Do her hips move at all?
- Does she come down heavily onto her feet? Does one foot strike harder than the other?
- Do her feet turn in, or turn out?
- How would you characterize her overall "energy"?
- Now everyone in the group "takes on" her walk. Follow her in the circle. Don't judge her walk, simply take it on and imitate it.
- Mirror her movements, her energy, her style.
- Watch her from head to toe, as a totality. Take that on yourself.
- How does her walk feel in your body?
- It may feel slightly unnatural to begin with, but will feel more authentic as you work with it.
- Each person walks in turn.
- When it's your turn, walk as you do habitually.
- Then see if you can slowly become conscious of what you are doing, without changing it.
- Watch the others as you continue to move. See them take on your walk. It's like watching several mirrors at once. You may see things reflected from your walk that you aren't aware of, or don't feel, or maybe are only dimly aware of. It can be a real awakening.

Imitating Animals

This is my variation on the classic animal exercise, which helps to train your eyes and brings you to very specific behaviors. Of course, an animal's wants and needs are primal and particular—that comes through in their movements. That same primal and particular quality will show in your movements when you use some of these techniques in your performances.

- Find a video of an animal you find interesting. If you can find more than one video of the same kind of animal, so much the better.
- Take your time watching the video. Watch it a number of times.
- Don't rush to the imitation. First gather information.
- Imitate the details that are easiest for you first. It might be the tempo or speed of movement, a movement quality, or certain idiosyncratic motions you relate to in some way.
- Begin to get a sense of the totality of the animal. How it seems to think and function.
- How does the animal use its head and neck?
- Do you notice its head leading, and its body following?
- What is the overall coordination of its body?
- How does its coordination relate to your coordination? Is it similar? Or different? Both similar and different?
- Use your instincts as well as your nonanalytic skills. Mirror what it is doing.
- How does it feel to move like this animal: physically and emotionally?
- What would this animal be like if it were a person? Would you be drawn to it?
- Imagine being this animal in its natural habitat. Use some of the work you did in the circles of attention exercise.
- Stand comfortably and transform yourself from the animal into a person who shares some of that animal's characteristics. Take a human stance influenced by the animal's.
- Begin to move and carry out activities as that person. Someone watching you probably wouldn't know you were basing your behavior on an animal.
- Can you imagine if this person is married? With children? What her job might be?
- How would you describe this person's movement and state of mind?

Imitating a Friend or Family Member

It's often best not to let people close to you know that you are "working off them" or *personalizing a character* based on some of their traits. It might make them uncomfortable, self-conscious, or taken advantage of. Consider keeping it to yourself. If you don't mention it, they won't know what you're working on. You could also use a photo or video of your chosen person as a visual cue.

- Observe your friend or family member without letting her know you are observing her. Be subtle.
- How does she stand? Walk? Move in general?
- Make sure you don't judge her for her habits. This is especially important with someone you are close to.
- When you're alone, begin to move as this person moves.
- Go through a number of everyday movements and activities, as she would.
- Choose a different activity, maybe something you've never seen her do before. How would she do it?
- Then choose something a little outrageous and do it as your friend/family member would do. Fight a dragon. Storm a castle. Perform on a late-night talk show. How would the person you observed behave?
- Take notes in your mind-body journal.

Mixing Your Influences

This is something that actors do unconsciously all the time. In this exercise, I suggest you try it consciously. Especially when you're in rehearsal for a play or about to start a film, your mind is constantly casting about, looking for people, places, and things that relate to the project. This is one way to do it purposely.

- Choose a character you're working on.
- Think about people you might use to help "personalize" that character.
- Take some gestures and movement characteristics from different sources: family members, friends, colleagues, people you've seen on the street, and other sources.

- Start with one aspect from one person—her walk, for example.
- Once you feel confident in that one aspect, add another from a different person.
- When you feel comfortable, add other aspects from other people.
- Try working with them all at once.
- Once you've got it in a way that works for you, try other movements as your character.
- Pick up a script and read with this use of the self.
- Try moving around, gesturing, behaving as the character as you read.
- If you like, improvise as the character, trying out this use of yourself.
- Later in the day, when you're doing other things, you can occasionally tune back in to this character, take her on for a few minutes at a time, and "try her out." It's like test-driving a car. You find your way into what works for you.

Silent Movie

Sometimes it's a good idea to get out of yourself and into something completely different. Take big chances and do something extravagant. Why not go there occasionally? It can help open something up inside of you, and you can then apply what you find to more subtle, contemporary work. What's fun about silent movies is that the acting technique was so different in the early twentieth century—it was based on the acting style used in very large theaters with no amplification, so often the actors were extravagant in the way they performed.

- Watch some clips from old silent movies.
- Find some that you like, or actors that appeal to you.
- Center yourself through your Alexander thoughts and breathing.
- Allow yourself to take on some of the characteristics of the performer you are observing.
- Take on some of her movements, her gestures, her sensibility, and her "style." For her, it is *real*. See if you can commit to it, and have it be real for you, too.
- How does this make you feel? Ridiculous? If so, see if you can stop watching yourself.
- You may feel oddly released by taking on something so unfamiliar, so unlike your daily life.
- Afterward, ask yourself if there is something useful you can take away from the experience that can be fruitfully applied to your current contemporary acting work.

Television

I live in New York City. There are "big personalities" on every corner. Every week I see something so dramatic on the street I think "If you saw that in a movie people wouldn't believe it." Finding the reality in a situation that seems exaggerated or hyperdramatic is an intriguing acting problem. Finding the real person inside someone who seems a bit of a "character" at first is an enriching thing to do. You'll bring many more facets to an "extreme" role, and learn something about human nature at the same time.

- Find a program that catches your eye on television: a reality show, talk show, singing competition, comedy, or drama. Hone in on one or two of the people on the program who intrigue you in some way.
- Observe how they do what they do: how they talk, what their body language is, how they move, and what their "energy" is. What is your overall sense of them?
- "Become" one of them. See what it's like to be a talk-show host, a reality-show contestant, a lawyer in a prime-time drama, or a singing contestant from a small town.
- *Resist commenting on the character*, especially if she is very different from you. Play her reality.
- Find her movement, her gestures, her way of being.
- Pick up a script and read some lines in her voice, even if the lines are not appropriate for her. Read as she would read.
- What would happen if you put the character in a situation she wouldn't normally be in? The singing contestant has to address the United Nations, for instance. Or a hair stylist from a reality show is elected president of the United States. What would she do? How would she behave? Let your imagination run with it.

A Movie Star from the Past

Now's your chance to be a vintage film star. If at all possible, do the exercise with a colleague, or, better yet, a group. You'll feel supported in exploring a whole other technique. Know that the acting style from the past is very different from today's, and that actors have always tried to be realistic within the confines of their time period and style. No actor sets out to be unconvincing. Also, it's not often today that you can be this extravagant with a character. You can really run with it playing the villain, the sweet and slightly helpless heroine, or the dashing young scientist who also flies airplanes and rescues animals and gets the bad guy in the end.

- Find a movie star from the distant past: 1920s–1940s. Choose one who interests you.
- If you like, ask your friends who know something about classic films which star from back then you remind them of.
- Watch the actor's films online. Study her.
- Notice what she wears, what seems to motivate her, what is striking about her.
- Once you have a sense of her, begin to let your personality merge with hers.
- Start with anything that might be similar between the two of you: height, face, ways of moving, a certain accessibility to emotion, and so on. Then begin to work on the things that feel slightly less familiar to you: her grandiosity, gracefulness, or kittenish quality.
- Let yourself "go there" and have fun.
- Even if, from your point of view, some of the acting is weak or flat-out bad, commit to it and go all the way with it. See if you can go with the style and panache of that period.

A Current Actor

In a way, this may be the most challenging of the imitation exercises. A prominent actor could be an intimidating subject to work off of. But don't get concerned about doing a completely accurate imitation. Simply use her as a person to work from.

- Choose a current prominent actor or movie star. Either someone people say you resemble in some way or someone you would like to work on.
- Watch videos of her online.
- Study the way she talks, walks, moves, and uses herself. What kind of roles does she usually play? How does she look? What kind of films does she appear in?
- Also study still photos, and read any interviews with her online to get an overall sense of her.
- What tempo-rhythms does she tend to use? How does she interact with the other performers? Do many of her characters tend to share certain characteristics? What are they?

- What do you have in common with the actor? The roles she plays?
- What differences might there be?
- In addition to her vocal habits, what do her breathing patterns tend to be?
- Begin by imitating something simple about her, something you can do easily.
- Add other small things that you notice, that you are able to replicate.
- If it helps you, choose music that seems to "fit" her, and work on her use to that music.
- Play back parts of the video a number of times, and imitate those brief sections as well as you can, without getting overly worried about it.
- Piece together small sections of the video, so that eventually you are able to imitate at least a minute of the video.
- If possible, find some sections of dialogue from some of her famous movies online. Read the dialogue "as her."
- Find a scene from a famous film with two people in it. Get a colleague to rehearse with you. Go at it as best you can, attempting to imitate the scene in the way it was played originally. See what feelings get stimulated in you by working in this way.
- Try the scene again, exaggerating all the actor's mannerisms.
- Do the scene again, staying with the same intentions and motivations, but take it to the other extreme and whisper the lines.
- Finally, play the scene as realistically and subtly as you can.

9

Using Voice and Movement to Stimulate the Mind-Body

We are mind-body-emotional beings. It all works together as a totality. People try to separate parts of themselves into different categories: "physical," "mental," and "spiritual." We do ourselves a disservice when we attempt to divide ourselves in this way. When you are working with your body and your voice to help explore and find a character, these two aspects of yourself work in tandem with your emotions: *it's not possible to separate them.* That's why a particularly good performance feels so satisfying—because everything works together as a unity: mind-body-breath-voice-emotions-connection-with-other-performers-and-the-audience. You see I had to coin a phrase for it, because it doesn't exist in our language. Some might say it's like when you "feel one with the Universe," the way you feel after you've gone out for a good run or come back from swimming. The endorphins are coursing through your body, you feel healthy and fit, alive and released in your body, at the top of your game, and in tune with everything around you.

Think about it this way: Should you forget your body when you're singing? It's perhaps best not to when singing one of the high notes in *Wicked*. When you're doing something "spiritual," like meditating, is it a good idea to forget about breathing? No: in fact, in most Eastern spiritual practices, the first thing they ask you to think about is your breathing. If you are doing something that is most obviously "physical," like Hamlet's sword fight with Laertes, should the actor forget about his emotions? Probably not, as they motivate the fight. It's best to attempt to keep all the aspects of yourself in mind as much as possible.

The exercises below, which deal with your breathing, voice, and movement, are not "external" exercises. *They are an integral part of who you are*, and what you are bringing to the role you're playing. Sometimes discovering a sound or rhythm in your voice and speech, a breathing pattern, or a way of moving or gesturing will give you psychological insight into your character. Why does she walk that way? Why does she pull away from people when they touch her? Why does she look down when people say she is pretty? These are all part of the character's *behavior*, which is the most honest part of how human beings are. People often say things that are shy of the truth for one reason or another. Often they want certain things to be true—but the body never lies. There is a *language of the body*. How you stand, how you move, how you gesture, how you touch other people, when you choose to be still, the parts of you that you're cut off from—these all say something undeniable about you.

Working with these exercises will often bring new insights to your thinking habits as well. Sometimes "thinking" gets a bad rap in the theater and film world. You hear a lot of directors and others tell actors, "Don't think too much." "You're trapped in your head." "Stop thinking. Pretend you're stupid." I know what they mean. You don't want to overintellectualize, ruminate, or compulsively worry about things. That doesn't help your acting. But when I use the word "thinking," I mean it in a different way. By "thought," I mean a simple, clear intention: "This is what I want. I want to give the best performance I can, through using myself in the best possible way, mind-body-emotion, all together." Or "I want to breathe easily, use myself well, and let go." Your thought-intension can be as simple as that.

PART ONE: Lying-Down Exercises

Humming Yourself

This exercise is not about singing, or even "sustained tone." It's about releasing what's inside of you and letting it go—out into the world. I call this exercise Humming Yourself because I see it as much more than just humming on a note. Your voice is very, very personal. No one else has one just like it. To create a sound within yourself, a hum, is a preparation not only to release an open, phonated sound but also to allow who you are to be revealed and escape out into the world. It's important not to worry about it or manipulate your sound. Sometimes when people think, "Oh, I'm going to sing," they tense up and do all kinds of things to "create the sound." You don't need to do any of that. Dare to keep it very simple. Focus on the vibration in your body, and stay connected to your air. When you open your mouth, try not to do anything differently from when you are humming: the process is the same. The only difference is you open your mouth. This keeps the onset clear. When you perform this exercise by "allowing" rather than "trying," you can sometimes feel naked. You're allowing your authentic self to be heard.

- Lie down in constructive rest. Paperback book under your head. Knees bent, or lower legs bent and resting on a chair. Hands rest on your lower ribs.
- Think the Alexander thoughts: *Neck free to allow your head go forward and out, torso to lengthen and widen.*
- Do three blowing out the candles.
- Then three whispered "ah"s.
- Hum somewhere near the center of your vocal range.
- Keep your humming light and easy.
- Sense the vibrations in your face, forehead, around your nose, cheekbones, and jaw. If you like, use your hands to feel it.
- Choose a slightly higher note. Hum on that, light and easy.
- Continue to be aware of the vibration in your face. Also sense the vibration in your chest.
- Choose a higher note to hum on lightly.
- Feel the vibration in your face, chest, rib cage, and back. Remember the idea that your whole body is naturally a resonating chamber. You don't have to "make it happen."
- Choose a note in the lower part of your voice to hum.
- Be aware of the vibration in your face, chest, back, and rib cage. See if you can sense small vibrations even in your arms, legs, hands, and feet.
- Hum another note in the lower part of your voice. A little louder this time. But you don't need to force anything. Simply the thought of being louder will let it happen.
- Hum on your center pitch again. Even a little louder.
- In the middle of humming, open your mouth easy into a sung "ah."
- *Don't worry about what it sounds like*, just allow the sound out.
- Repeat on the center pitch. Hum, opening into an "ah."
- A third time, this time even a little louder. Remember not to worry about the sound.
- Pause and breathe quietly.
- See if you can sense the remnants of vibration in your face, chest, and whole body.
- Hum on your center pitch, open into a nice loud (but not pushed) "ah." Remember not to be concerned with how it sounds. If there are cracks, breaks, or gravel in your voice, don't be concerned with it. The voice is working itself out. It's temporary.
- Continue up the scale, one note at a time. Hum, opening into a big, solid "ah." Then come down the scale in the same way.

Chanting

Chanting—the transition from whispering or humming into singing or speech—isn't something you do very much unless you happen to be a monk. That's what makes it fruitful as an exercise. Since you don't do it often, there are fewer habits associated with it. Chanting also feels "safe." It feels easy. It doesn't frighten or intimidate, as singing can do. It's similar in certain ways to "speak-singing," or what the Germans call *Sprechgesang*, a technique in opera recitative whereby certain pitches are sung with very loose articulation. There is also Sprechstimme, which is even closer to speech because no particular pitches are stressed.

- Take yourself through the previous exercise in preparation for this one. Leave your body "up and out" rather than pulling down and in.
- Hum on your center pitch.
- In the middle of humming it, open your mouth and chant the word "one," then return to humming. It will sound like "Mm—one—mm."
- Then hum, and lead into chanting, "Mm—one, two—mm."
- Stay easy in your body and breathing.
- Then "Mm—one, two, three—mm."
- "Mm—one, two, three, four—mm."
- "Mm—one, two, three, four, five—mm."
- Then try it without the hum before the chanting. Remember to stay easy as you chant one through five. Allow one word to elide into the next. Almost think of it as one long word. Let the articulation be loose.
- Repeat several times. *Easy in the neck, head balanced at the top of your spine, body long and easy.* Stay "on your air" easily.
- Chant to ten. Staying easy in yourself.
- Repeat several times. Neck and shoulders loose. Easy breathing.
- Allow the sound out of yourself, into the room, into the world.

Floor-Supported Sound

So often people try to overcontrol or manipulate their sound. It's not possible with this movement, which is kind of primal. The key is not to worry about what you sound like. Leave your jaw, tongue, neck, and shoulders free as you roll. You may even be pleasantly surprised at the authentic sounds that come out of you as you roll.

- Lie on your back, a paperback book under your head, knees bent.
- Think through your Alexander thoughts. Free breathing.
- Allow a hum to buzz in your face, throat, and chest.
- Do that a few times.
- Hum on an "Mmm" sound. Open your mouth into a hearty "ah." It will sound like "Mmmmmmahhhhhh."
- Repeat a few times.
- Roll onto your side into a loose fetal position.
- Hum on an "Mmm" sound. Open your mouth into a hearty "ah." It will sound like "Mmmmmmahhhhhh."
- Roll onto your other side and repeat.
- Roll gently from side to side. Make the sound as you roll from side to side.
- The physical motion will help keep your vocal sound free. Don't worry if the pitch jangles a bit as you move.

Nursery Rhymes

Nursery rhymes are worth working on, especially as a bridge from counting into regular speech. You know the rhyme so well that you don't have to think about what you're saying. The words are almost automatic, so you're able to focus on your Alexander directions, remembering to stay connected to your breathing.

- Work through some of the exercises above.
- *Leave your neck easy, your head balanced and poised, your torso lengthened. Your breath free.*
- Say:

> Hickory, dickory, dock,
> The mouse ran up the clock.
> The clock struck one,
> The mouse ran down,
> Hickory, dickory, dock.

- Repeat a few times. Leave your body free, easy in your breathing, letting all the words flow one into the next, without worrying too much about the meaning of the words.
- Try speaking it louder. But leave yourself just as free.
- Speak it on different pitches. Go up and down the scale of your speaking voice.
- Whisper the rhyme.

- See if you can almost shout the rhyme, but with an easy throat, jaw, and tongue.
- Speak the rhyme one last time, in your normal voice.
- Try different nursery rhymes, if you like.
- Then speak a few normal sentences. What does it feel like to speak after the exercise?

Poetry—Emily Dickinson

Emily Dickinson is one of the greatest American poets, and a genius in her brevity and discernment of feeling. Her poetry lends itself to straightforward and unadorned interpretation. Her sincerity invites the same in you.

- Think your Alexander thoughts.
- Whisper "ah" three times.
- Allow your breath to be low and slow.
- Whisper "ah" three more times.
- Recite or read:

> It's all I have to bring today –
> This, and my heart beside –
> This, and my heart, and all the fields –
> And all the meadows wide –
> Be sure you count – should I forget
> Some one the sum could tell –
> This, and my heart, and all the Bees
> Which in the Clover dwell.

- Return to your Alexander thoughts. Free your breathing.
- Think about the meaning of the words. Recite or read it again.
- Speak it a third time, thinking about freeing yourself; think about the meaning and sound of the words.
- Allow your mind-body to release into a deep place that can speak poetry such as this.

Poetry—Shakespeare

Ah, Shakespeare. The main thing is not to be intimidated by him. Read his words over as many times as needed to get used to their sound and meaning. He knows just when to give you time to breathe, and the rhythm and cadence of what he's written often lets you know what to emphasize. Suggest to yourself that you have just as much right to speak his verse as anyone else. This is one of his "simplest" sonnets, in that it's not difficult to understand, but is certainly profound. See what you can find in it, and what you can bring to it.

- Center your mind-body.
- *Let your neck be free, to let your head go forward and out, to let your torso be long and wide. Arms and legs to release away from your body.*
- Allow the breath to be low and slow.
- Don't worry about how you are saying the poetry. Let yourself be free and recite, or read the words:

    Shall I compare thee to a summer's day?
    Thou art more lovely and more temperate.
    Rough winds do shake the darling buds of May,
    And summer's lease hath all too short a date.
    Sometime too hot the eye of heaven shines,
    And often is his gold complexion dimmed;
    And every fair from fair sometime declines,
    By chance, or nature's changing course, untrimmed;
    But thy eternal summer shall not fade,
    Nor lose possession of that fair thou ow'st,
    Nor shall death brag thou wand'rest in his shade,
    When in eternal line to Time thou grow'st.
    So long as men can breathe, or eyes can see,
    So long lives this, and this gives life to thee.

- Return to easy, even breathing.
- Say the words again, taking an easy breath whenever you need it. Take your time with it, and be aware of the meaning of the words, without letting that tighten you up.
- Say the words a third time, this time giving your attention to the sound of the words more than their meaning.
- Put it all together. Speak the words, being aware of yourself, your breathing, the words' meaning and their sound.
- See how the poetry resonates in your body after you finish speaking.
- Return to yourself, freeing your body and your breathing.

PART TWO: Exercises for a Group

Telling a Story

Some actors are surprisingly shy about "being themselves" in front of a group. They feel more comfortable in the cloak of a character. But you don't have to be witty or intelligent or entertaining. Simply tell a story and see what happens if you "leave yourself alone."

- Have the group form a semicircle.
- Stand in front of the group.
- See if you can stay as easy as possible in your body and your breathing.
- Sense the space between the top of your head and your feet.
- Sense the space around you and the audience in front of you.
- Notice if you become slightly defensive, apologetic, or self-conscious.
- Leave yourself physically and emotionally as open as possible as you tell the story.
- Talk about anything. What you did yesterday. What you're going to do tomorrow. Something interesting that happened to you recently.
- See if you can focus on telling your story, rather than worrying about your audience, or what they're thinking or feeling.
- Stay with the idea of releasing up and out as you tell the story.
- Leave your breath easy.
- Notice how you feel in your mind-body after you tell your story.
- Note how you react psycho-physically as others tell their stories. Can you stay easy in your body and breathe as they speak?

Tossing a Yawn

This is a fun exercise. It gets your imagination, breath, and body all moving together. It's good to do as a warm-up before a rehearsal. It keeps things light. You can also try tossing an imaginary helium ball back and forth.

- Stand across from your partner.
- Both of you give two yawns.
- One of you yawns and uses your hand to "capture" the yawn and toss it to your partner.

- The partner "catches" the yawn, puts it in her mouth, and yawns.
- She uses her hand to "capture" it and toss it back. Do this several times.
- One of you yawns, which turns into a hum, which turns into a sung "ah." Toss the sung "ah" across to your partner.
- Both of you repeat this several times.
- Change the pitch of your sung note.
- Physically alter how you're throwing: high, low, fast, slow.

Speaking across the Room

This is not about "vocal projection." Probably that phrase should be dropped from the theatrical lexicon. Something about the word "projection" makes most people want to push and force. The purpose of the exercise, and speaking on a stage, is to communicate. This is a way of playing around with what you need to do in order to communicate effectively with people at various distances and still maintain a good use of yourself.

- Stand across from your partner.
- Think: *Neck free, head forward and up, torso lengthening and widening.*
- Allow your breath to be low and slow.
- Do three blowing out the candles.
- Say the first lines of classic poems to each other. First one person says the line, then the other repeats it. Then move onto the next line.
- Here are some lines you can use:

  She walks in beauty, like the night
  Of cloudless climes and starry skies

  ...

  Some have won a wild delight,
  By daring wilder sorrow;
  Could I gain thy love to-night,
  I'd hazard death to-morrow.

  ...

  Beds to the front of them,
  Beds to the right of them,
  Beds to the left of them,
  Nobody blundered.

...

In Xanadu did Kubla Khan
A stately pleasure-dome decree

...

The shell of objects inwardly consumed
Will stand, till some convulsive wind awakes;
Such sense hath Fire to waste the heart of things,
Nature, such love to hold the form she makes.

...

What was he doing, the great god Pan,
Down in the reeds by the river?

...

Four seasons fill the Measure of the year;
Four seasons are there in the mind of Man.

...

- Use a physical action with the line when you say it. Toss lines to each other. Throw them up to the ceiling, or out the window. Walk around the room. Dance the poem as you say it to your partner.
- Try using different parts of your voice, different registers. Try different speeds and rhythms.
- Remember to keep breathing easily.
- Try moving farther and farther away from each other. You don't need to shout or push. Simply have your intention be to share the poem with your partner.
- Try singing or chanting the lines to each other.
- If you like, speak some of the lines in unison.
- Finally, stand still and be quiet in yourself.
- Speak the lines very simply to each other.

PART THREE: Sound and Movement Exercises

Evolution Sequence

Crawling is a unique activity you rarely practice as an adult. Like walking backward, it's an activity that won't have many habits associated with it. You may even have to think a little bit about how to locomote. Having four supports is good for your back and helps promote its lengthening. This position also encourages freedom in the hips, which tends to release you through the lower back.

- Lie flat on your stomach. Arms by your side.
- Your head leads your spine into length. Let your body be supported by the floor.
- Sense your own breathing.
- Bring yourself up onto all fours.
- Have your hands underneath your shoulders. Your knees underneath your hip sockets.
- Allow your head to be balanced at the top of your spine, torso elongated.
- In this position, your head leads forward and out, in the direction you will be moving.
- Check that you're not stiffening at the base of your skull, and compressing your head onto your neck.
- Crawl forward: your head leading, your body following.
- Cross-crawl: your knee comes forward, and the opposite hand comes forward in tandem.
- Crawl around the room. *Your head leads, your body follows.*
- Let your eyes look down at each hand as it comes forward. That will help to keep your head from compressing back onto your neck.
- Try crawling backward. In this case, the tailbone leads and the rest of the body follows.
- Switch back and forth between crawling forward and backward.
- Keep the motion flowing. If you need to, come onto your haunches to pause.
- Begin to hum as you crawl.
- Let the movement and sound work together. Leave your breath easy.
- Allow the gentle motion of the crawling to encourage the vibration throughout your whole body, especially your face, chest, and back.
- Kneel and bring one foot through and onto the floor. Bring yourself up into standing.
- Give yourself a moment to readjust to standing.
- Think up and out through your torso. *Think of your head leading your body in an upward direction.*
- Walk around the room. The head leads, the body follows, as in crawling.
- Continue to sense the ease that you found in your crawling.
- Think of your knees moving forward, as they did in crawling.
- Allow for the cross-pattern reflex, as you did in crawling. Your arms swing in opposition to the knees coming forward.
- Let there be freedom in the shoulders and hips.
- Let the humming lead into "Mmmaahs."
- Sense the power of free movement together with free sound.
- *Allow your neck to be free, your head to go forward and up, your body to follow* as you walk.
- Speak some nursery rhymes and poetry in tandem with your movement.

Sculpting the Air

It's sometimes useful to read nondramatic material out loud. It takes the worry off characterization and drama and puts the focus squarely on storytelling and communication. The sculpting movements distract you in a positive way from worrying about reading and what you're doing. It's also using a creative side of your brain and tying it in with your communication. When you come to reading again without movement, something has been loosened inside you, and this is reflected in how you read.

- Stand comfortably, thinking your Alexander thoughts, allowing your breath to be low and slow.
- Read out loud from a news source.
- As you read, or after you read, see if you can notice any physical or vocal habits you may have.
- Does your neck tighten? Place your hand there so you can check.
- Does your head pull back and get heavy on the back of your neck?
- Do your shoulders stiffen and lift? Or do they pull forward? Check with your hands.
- What about your back? Does it stiffen or slump as you read?
- Remind yourself to say no to your tension habits and to gently lengthen and widen.
- Have the intention of remaining poised as you read.
- Read again.
- Stay as physically, vocally, and mentally free as you can as you read.
- Let your hands move as you read. You can start by almost "conducting yourself."
- Allow your motions to grow larger.
- Let the movements support what you are doing as you read.
- Begin to "sculpt the air" with your hands, almost like you are creating sculpture with your hands out of the words you are saying.
- Or "paint the air," as though it's a three-dimensional canvas.
- Focus on the physical movements, so the words are almost secondary.
- Allow your body to follow the motions you're making. You're creating a three-dimensional art object that comes out of your creative impulses.

Using Music in a Monologue

Somehow, using music in a monologue keeps you feeling safe. It's there to support you, and you feel less prone to push your emotions. Increased freedom in the body, breathing, voice, and feelings is what we're looking for. Let the music carry you along. It's a way you can let go of anything you may be holding back inside.

- Find a monologue that you would like to memorize or read.
- Put on music that you feel is appropriate for the monologue.
- Read the monologue very simply, with the music playing.
- Allow yourself to be in "the Alexander zone."
- See how the music affects you emotionally and physically.
- Read the monologue again, allowing yourself to be moved by the music. Give yourself permission.
- When you're done, pause. Forget about the monologue for the moment.
- Listen to the music.
- Let it work on you.
- Dare to let yourself be exposed.
- Then read.

Dancing a Monologue or Scene

This is about connecting with the nonintellectual part of you and allowing your body to move from your inner impulses. See if you can let yourself go there. If you can, something new will happen to your monologue. It's easiest if you have a monologue memorized for this exercise.

- Put music on that is appropriate for the monologue.
- Stand. Leave yourself still and quiet, listening to the music.
- Then listen to it a second time.
- Remind yourself that you don't need to "act." Just respond to the music and what the words are about.
- Begin the monologue in a simple way.
- Allow your body to sway to the music.
- Don't worry about what you look like. Don't worry about how to move.
- Let your movements get a little bigger.

- When you finish the monologue, turn the music up.
- Let your body move to the music.
- Don't worry about "doing it right."
- Allow your movements to build.
- Don't work out what you're going to do. Just do it.
- Continue to dance around the room as you do the monologue.
- Let it be large. Take big chances. Go a little crazy with it.
- When you've finished, stand still. Continue to let the music play.
- Do the monologue without dancing. You can move if you want, but you don't have to. This time be authentic; be respectful to the text.
- If you have a brave partner, do a scene this way together.

Silent Dance

Here is an opportunity for you to choreograph movements that fit the inner life of the writing and what the author is trying to say. Sometimes movement can express more than words, or express it in another way. Explore and see what you find that you can use when you perform the monologue in the usual way.

- Stand quietly.
- Think about your monologue. Who the character is. What the situation is. What your character wants, and what she is doing.
- Think about *the moment before* the monologue begins.
- Think the first line of the monologue.
- Then begin to move.
- You don't speak.
- Act out the monologue through movement only.
- You can act the monologue physically, line by line. Or you can do a series of movements that symbolize the overall meaning for you.
- Let the movements be as large or as small as you feel.
- At the end of the piece, see if you can find one psychological gesture that sums up the monologue for you.
- If you like, you can do the exercise again, this time with sound. You can hum, sing, make random noises, or speak gibberish. Just don't speak the words as written.

PART THREE

Putting It All Together

10

Auditions, Rehearsals, and Performances

Acting is not just memorizing and reciting words. It's a complex process of absorbing what a writer is trying to say about the character and the story, and using all aspects of yourself to bring that off the page and into three-dimensional life. In a great piece of writing there is always a theme that encapsulates what the writer is attempting to say about the world of the play or film, and also the world at large. It's part of the actor's job to understand what the story is, with all its ramifications, and how you fit into it. Your contribution is to approach your character nonjudgmentally, to understand her wants and needs, and to *embody* that. This involves deeply submerging yourself into the material on multiple levels: intellectual, emotional, physical, vocal, even spiritual, if you think about things that way. This is a tall order—especially when a project is being put together quickly, as can often be the case.

It's important for you to do all the homework you can to keep yourself in good acting shape, for whenever your opportunities arise. We've laid out many ways that you can work on your breathing, voice, body, and feelings. Continue to work with these "basics." They're called basics because you'll need them over and over again in your personal and professional spheres. Honing these skills will engage you for the rest of your life.

Now you'll want to begin to think about how to directly apply your newfound knowledge to actual acting work. Whether it's an independent film, a play on a large stage, a commercial, an industrial film, or a blockbuster, your motivation is the same—to bring all you can to the table.

PART ONE: Gathering Information about Yourself

Reading Aloud

This is one of the most elemental ways you can work with yourself. Taking up new and different kinds of text will help you hone your reading skills and make you increasingly comfortable doing it. Bringing your mind-body habits into your consciousness will help you expand what feels possible for you. You'll discover what inhibits you psycho-physically, and learn that you can change it, so that working in front of a microphone, doing cold readings, and voice-overs will become a pleasure. Try this exercise both sitting and standing. You may have different habits in each.

- Read aloud from the different sources: a script, narration from a novel, and current news. Each is a different kind of writing. You may react to them in different ways, both psychologically and physically.
- Read as you would habitually, without thinking about it.
- What do you notice about yourself as you read? What habits are you aware of?
- Do you slump over the script or reading material? Does your neck jut forward, and your head pull back? Do your shoulders pull forward, or pull up toward your ears (or both)?
- What about your back? Does it stiffen? Does your breathing get more shallow, or more labored?
- Even your arms and legs may get into the act. Do they shake? Or become stiff?
- What happens to you psychologically? Do you worry before you start reading? Do you "listen to yourself" hypercritically? Do you start shaking?
- Are you not quite in the moment?
- You can also do this exercise with a partner whom you trust.
- Observe what your partner does when she reads.
- What does she do with her body, her arms, and her breathing? Does her neck stiffen? Does her head compress down onto her spine?
- Are certain things more obvious with different kinds of texts?
- Is her voice similar to when she speaks in everyday life? Or do certain habits become more obvious when she reads? What happens during the onset—the moment your partner takes a breath to read?
- Give each other constructive feedback.

Reading in Front of Colleagues

It can sometimes be surprisingly stressful to read in front of colleagues, even people you like and trust. It's a common issue; there's something revealing about it. But the more you do it, the easier it gets and the less concerned you are about making a mistake or "making a good impression." Note that your habits may tend to come in a bit more strongly than they do when you work on your own or with one acting partner.

- Stand in front of a group of colleagues to read. Read short selections from a script, a novel, and from the news. (This exercise can also be done with singing.)
- After you read, make note of your mind-body habits.
- Were you able to keep your focus on what you were reading? Were you concerned about what you looked like, or sounded like? Did you feel self-conscious?
- Did you shake? Were you comfortable in your stance? What happened with your body when you were reading?
- Did you feel easy when reading? Or were you aware of tightening in your throat, or restriction in your breathing? What was your experience of your own voice? When you are reading the news or a novel, are you able to "be yourself" or do you feel like you must be someone else?
- Get feedback from your colleagues. Keep it positive and constructive. They can also mention things they felt you did well.
- Observe your colleagues as they read. Give them constructive feedback.

Discomfort

This exercise is a challenge! To deliberately put yourself in a position where you are out of your comfort zone is not easy. But maybe this is a metaphor for life in the performing arts. There may be many moments where you are uncertain in your professional life. The most helpful thing is to come back to basics: release your mind-body and breathe.

- Try this exercise with a trusted colleague or friend—so it's a "safe space."
- Do something that takes you out of your comfort zone. Sing. Do a monologue you don't know well or haven't performed yet. Play a character you wouldn't ordinarily play, or one that makes you a little uncomfortable.

- How do you feel right before you perform it? What do you notice about yourself, psycho-physically?
- What happens to your breathing?
- Ask your colleague to notice what happens right at the start. And what happens overall.
- After you perform, if you are able, take note of what you've done. Sometimes, if you are uncomfortable, it's challenging to be clear on what happened or for you to be objective about it.
- Gather information from your colleague about what she noticed.
- If you like, try it again, and see if you can be a bit easier with things. Especially on judging your own performance.

PART TWO: Recording Yourself

Freeing Your Vocal Mechanism

Before you record yourself on audio it's a good idea to bring yourself into the "Alexander zone." If you have time, lie down in constructive rest and spend ten to fifteen minutes there, about an hour or forty-five minutes before you record, so there's time to get back into "performance mode" after lying down. Focusing on your jaw, tongue, face, and neck will help to release and gently energize the area, so that you can use your authentic sound.

- Stand with ease. One foot slightly in front of the other. Arms easily at your side.
- Think your Alexander thoughts: *Let your neck be free, to let your head release forward and up, to let your torso lengthen and widen, to let your arms and legs release away from your body.*
- Check in with your neck—front, back, and sides. Ask it to be free.
- Let your jaw muscles be easy.
- Ask your tongue, especially deep at the root above the larynx, to let go.
- Check in with your shoulders: ask them to be open and wide.
- Use a few fingers to massage your jaw. Go in small circles. Then press gently straight in on the jaw muscles.
- Gently massage the very base of your tongue, just above your larynx.
- Yawn naturally (not in a forced way) three times. This helps to open up the throat and gently raise the soft palette. You don't have to make it happen, it happens of its own accord. It also calms the fight-or-flight response.

- Place your released hand on the front of your neck, on either side of your larynx, to remind your neck to be free.
- Place your released hand on the back of your neck, at the base of your skull, to remind your head not to pull back and down, but to allow it to go forward and up.

Recording at Home

With repetition, this exercise will help you become familiar and comfortable with the whole process of recording. Your mind-body begins to associate acting with release instead of restriction and tightness.

- Stand in front of the microphone.
- Adjust the height of the microphone so it works for your height.
- Adjust the height of the music stand, with the script on it.
- Find a stance for yourself where you are neither too close nor too far away from the microphone or copy. You might consider putting one foot slightly in front of the other. This often helps to release your lower back.
- Have a pencil on the stand for notes.
- Test the microphone for sound quality and audibility.
- Think your Alexander guiding thoughts.
- Do three blowing out the candles. Then three whispered "ah"s.
- Check to make sure that you're not raising or rounding your shoulders.
- Ask yourself not to slump down through your torso.
- Ask yourself not to arch your lower back, or stiffen your legs.
- Let your torso be long. Allow your shoulders and chest to be wide. Let your lower back be soft. Allow your lower abdomen to be engaged to support your lower back. Allow your legs to be free, and release down toward the ground, away from your torso. Remind yourself to free your tongue and jaw.
- Read the script and record yourself.
- Stay as easy and free as possible in your body when you read. Keep your breath flowing.
- When you're finished recording, step away from the microphone.
- Remind yourself of your Alexander suggestions and your easy breathing.
- Listen to the playback. Note, nonjudgmentally, anything you would like to change.

Recording a Scene

This exercise can be useful for work in podcasts, dubbing a film, and even old radio plays that are performed live. Sometimes in these types of recording jobs, the director is looking for quick results. Ironically, one of the best ways to deliver that is to remain focused on the process.

- Find a way to position yourselves around the microphone, or, ideally, have one microphone for each person. Or one microphone for every two actors to share.
- Get yourself as comfortable as possible.
- Check if you tend to have any physical habits when grouped close to others.
- See if there's a way to be standing close without pulling in and down on yourself.
- Check to see if you "pick up on the group energy" or if you are able to "stay with yourself" in a constructive way.
- Take note if you compare yourself too much to the others in the group.
- See if you get concerned about "getting it right" or "nailing it" as opposed to just doing the work.
- Bring your focus to the process, as opposed to the result.
- Think through your Alexander suggestions, and remember your breathing in a way that isn't obvious, and doesn't draw attention to itself.
- When you're finished, listen to the playback.
- Listen to others, as well as yourself.
- Take note of what you liked, and what you might change.
- Record again.

Working in Front of a Still Camera

It's useful to try this exercise with a few friends if you can. It's great practice for recognizing shots that work for you and for the all-important issue of getting very familiar with the camera. You've heard it said about some performers that "the camera loves them." It's a quality that's hard to define. It's partly what you look like, what you wear, and how you present yourself. But a lot of it is how you interact with the camera.

- Have a friend photograph you.
- Do a "mock photo shoot" as if you are getting new headshots, or having a series of commercial print photos taken.
- Look online at photos you like: actors' headshots, advertising photos. Study the body language: try it on, and become comfortable with what feels good for you. Check out models and actors that are similar to you. Notice what they are wearing and what body positions they tend to use.
- Put together a choice of clothing as if you were having headshots taken. Have at least three changes of clothing. If you are doing a mock commercial print shoot, you'll need more clothing.
- If you can, plan to shoot some photos inside and some outside.
- How do you feel when you look into the camera?
- Is it intimidating? Off-putting? Are you a little afraid of it?
- Do you project something onto the camera?
- If you consider yourself a stage actor, are you more comfortable on a stage, and freeze a little when a camera is around?
- What happens to your body and your breathing when you stand in front of the camera?
- Are you able to stand in front of it, and remain breathing easily? (This will help release your eyes, and the muscles around your eyes.)
- Do you find yourself pulling yourself toward the camera, or are you comfortable allowing the camera to "come to you"?
- Look into the center of the lens of the camera, without pulling your eyes away.
- If it helps you, imagine someone you like or love in the lens.
- Keep breathing easily as you look into the lens. Make sure not to tense or freeze if you're asked to hold a position. Keep the position released.
- Keep "renewing" your energy for each shot. That doesn't mean being falsely "on"—simply communicate nonverbally with the camera each time.
- Rather than feeling you must suddenly turn into a "model," continue to think about yourself as an actor. For the commercial print shots, you can think of each of the shots as being a character, if that helps you—a young mother, a businesswoman, and so on.
- Invite the camera in, as if it were someone you trust, like, and admire. This will be reflected in your eyes and your body language.

Working in Front of a Video Camera

In front of a camera, you won't need to speak as loudly as you do on a stage, of course. Even if the camera is positioned far across the room, it's focused closely on your face, and the microphone will pick up what you're saying easily. It's a matter of staying as truthful and natural as possible. That's a simple concept, but takes some practice. Give yourself permission to experiment. When you get a job and there are lights everywhere, a more intimidating camera, other performers, and a crew, it can all get a bit distracting. Truthful and natural are the qualities to remember.

- Place a video camera where it can capture you and turn it on.
- Do some warm-ups in front of the camera, both to get you going and to allow you to feel less self-conscious in front of it.
- *Sense-poise-flow.* Do three blowing out the candles. Then three whispered "ah"s.
- Allow yourself to breathe in front of the camera.
- Try a few hums. Get the vibration going.
- Yawn twice to open up the throat and to calm the startle response.
- Count to five a few times. Then count to ten a few times. Get used to speaking in front of the camera.
- "Slate" yourself. That means you face the camera, look into it, and say your name. Read a poem, part of a novel, or a news report. Don't look into the camera.
- Try reading something else. This time look into the camera.
- Read something else. Stand if you aren't doing so already. And walk about as you read. Don't look into the camera this time.
- Return to your beginning position.
- Put down your reading material. Slate your name again.

Performing a Monologue in Front of a Camera

This takes the previous exercise a step further and ups the ante a bit.

- Choose a monologue that you know well.
- Spend a few moments connecting to your body and your air.
- Go through your Alexander directions and breathing. Make this part of your routine.
- When you're ready, let your friend know.
- Take a moment to think about your character's "moment before" and then begin.
- Perform the monologue.
- When you're done with the speech, take a few moments before you "break character." Sometimes strong emotions come through after you've finished a monologue, especially in your face.

- Stay easy in yourself as you watch the playback.
- Try not to be hypercritical of yourself. Just observe what's there.
- Make note of any adjustments you'd like to make.
- Remind yourself gently about sense-poise-flow.
- Then do the monologue again.
- If you trust your friend to be constructive, ask for her feedback on your comfort in front of the camera.

Performing a Scene in Front of the Camera

This exercise brings you the closest to what it's like on an actual set. You are performing a rehearsed scene with blocking with another actor. But it's still a safe environment for you to be able to try things out. If you feel yourself tightening up during the scene, take a break from shooting and spend a few moments doing a few of the exercises which help you to release. Remember, you're not looking for perfection. You're moving step by step in the direction you want to go.

- Choose a short scene that you and your acting partner will have memorized.
- Spend some time rehearsing, working out the moves you'd like to make. Working out the mechanics will first allow you to focus on your character's needs and emotions.
- Do a psycho-physical warm-up beforehand.
- Stay in the moment as best you can while you shoot the scene.
- Watch the playback. Discuss with your partner afterward whether there's anything you want to adjust.
- Shoot a second time. See how the two takes compare.

PART THREE: At-Home Warm-Ups

One-Minute Warm-Up

- Blow out the candle slowly, as long as you can. Ten seconds or more, if you can.
- Don't breathe in until you need to.

- Yawn twice.
- Stretch both of your arms up to the ceiling.
- Come up onto your toes.
- Reach up through your arms, allow your torso to lengthen.
- Come back to center.
- Roll your shoulders.
- Turn your head side to side, to loosen your neck.

Two-Minute Warm-Up

- Walk in a circle.
- Reverse, and walk the other way.
- Reverse. As you walk, raise and lower your arms toward the ceiling.
- Stand in place, in a wide stance.
- Reach up with one hand toward the ceiling, and grab an imaginary ring, and pull it down toward you. It resists a bit, so you need to pull.
- Pull with the other hand. Repeat three more times on each side.
- Come back to center.
- Open and close your mouth a few times. Move your tongue from side to side. Yawn.
- Stretch your arms out to either side.
- With your arms open, hum on an open-mouthed "ah."
- Repeat. Start with an open-mouth "ah," then open into a sung "ah."
- Let your arms float down.
- Chant from one to five. Then chant one to ten.
- Practice some boxing moves. Or powerful moves from martial arts.
- Make your movements strong but not tense.

Three-Minute Warm-Up

- Stand a few feet in front of a wall. Face the wall.
- Lunge forward. The front knee bent, the back leg is straight.
- With your arms stretched straight out in front of you, push against the wall.
- Leave your back lengthened. Check to make sure you don't arch your back.
- Bend your other knee forward, repeat the movement.

- Stand, centered, at your full height.
- Bring yourself into position of *mechanical advantage (monkey)*. That is a knee bend, with your torso leaning forward from your hips.
- Allow your head to lead your spine into the forward bend, as your knees bend forward.
- Check that your back doesn't hunch forward. It stays lengthened and widened. Check that your head is not retracted back and down.
- Staying in the position of mechanical advantage, place your hands on your lower back. Whisper "ah."
- Hum in the lower part of your voice. Feel the vibrations in your lower back with your hands.
- Continue to hum as you come back to standing. Change the pitch.
- Come back into the monkey position as you hum. Open into a sung "ah."
- Stand. Hum into a sung "ah."
- Bring your hands off your lower back.
- Count in a series of one to ten.
- As you count, float your arms out to the sides, up toward the ceiling, and down again. Repeat.
- As you continue to count, float your arms in front of you, up toward the ceiling, and down again. Repeat.
- Come back to center.
- As you continue counting, march. Swing your opposing arm up. If your left knee lifts, your right arm comes forward.
- Come to center.
- Count, as you go through a knee bend to leap up into a jump. Repeat several times.
- Come to center.
- Whisper "ah" three times.
- Sense-poise-flow.

Memorizing Lying Down

Constructive rest is one of the healthiest positions for your body and your breathing. It's also a deeply soothing place to be. Why not use it to keep yourself feeling calm and focused as you memorize your script?

- Lie down in constructive rest position.
- Remind yourself of the Alexander suggestions, and your breathing.
- Get yourself as quiet and released as possible.
- Put a large pillow on your stomach and a pillow under your head.
- Prop your script against the pillow on your stomach.
- You can now read your script in a very easy body position.
- As you read your script, keep your breathing easy. Check in to see that you're not tightening as you read.
- If you like, read some of the lines aloud.

Memorizing While Moving

Memorizing while moving is not the same as pacing. Pacing comes from discomfort and tension. You may also do this exercise while sitting or standing quietly, or try it with a friend helping you with your lines.

- Allow your body to be free: *Neck free, head poised forward and up, your torso long and wide.*
- Let your breathing be low and slow. Both this and your Alexander thoughts will help keep you from tightening while working on the script.
- Leave your arms without excessive tension, hold your script lightly.
- Check to make sure you don't slump down toward the page. Hold the script high enough so that you can see it easily at your full height.
- You can either move at random, or try out blocking for the scene.
- Leave your body easy as you move.
- If you catch yourself tightening up, pause for a moment, redirect your thinking, and continue. It will only take a split second, and anyone watching you wouldn't know what you were doing. It would not be "breaking character."
- Make one of your motivations in working on the script to maintain as much freedom as possible, so you can bring that freedom to your performance.

PART FOUR: Speech Warm-Ups

Thirty-Second Poetry Warm-Up

Over hill, over dale,
Through brush, through brier,
Over park, over pale,
Through flood, through fire,
I do wander everywhere,
Swifter than the moon's sphere;
And I serve the fairy queen,
To dew her orbs upon the green.
The cowslips tall her pensioners be:
In their gold coats spots you see;
Those be freckles live their savors.
I must go seek some dewdrops here
And hang a pearl in every cowslip's ear.

Forty-Five-Second Poetry Warm-Up

When the night wind howls
In the chimney cowls,
And the bat in the moonlight flies,
And the inky clouds,
Like funeral shrouds,
Sail over the midnight skies—
...
When the footpads quail
At the night-bird's wail,
And the black dogs bay at the moon,
Then is the spectre's holiday—
Then is the ghost's high noon!
...
Ha! Ha!
For then is the ghost's high noon!

One-Minute Poetry Warm-Up

Life, believe, is not a dream
So dark as sages say;
Oft a little morning rain
Foretells a pleasant day.
Sometimes there are clouds of gloom,
But these are transient all;
If the shower will make the roses bloom,
O why lament its fall?

…

Rapidly, merrily,
Life's sunny hours flit by,
Gratefully, cherrily,
Enjoy them as they fly!

…

What though Death at times steps in
And calls our Best away?
What though sorrow seems to win,
O'er hope, a heavy sway?
Yet hope again elastic springs,
Unconquered, though she fell;
Still buoyant are her golden wings,
Still strong to bear us well.
Manfully, fearlessly,
The day of trial bear,
For gloriously, victoriously,
Can courage quell despair!

Forty-Five-Second Prose Warm-Up

Let me begin with facts – bare, meagre facts, verified by books and figures, and of which there can be no doubt. I must not confuse them with experiences which will have to rest on my own observation or my memory of them. Last evening when the Count came from his room he began by asking me questions on legal matters and on the doing of certain kinds of business. I had spent the day wearily over books, and, simply to keep my mind occupied, went over some of the matters I had been examined in at Lincoln's Inn. There was a certain method in the Count's inquiries, so I shall try to put them down in sequence; the knowledge may somehow or some time be useful to me.

Fifty-Second Prose Warm-Up

It was the best of times, it was the worst of times, it was the age of wisdom, it was the age of foolishness, it was the epoch of belief, it was the epoch of incredulity, it was the season of Light, it was the season of Darkness, it was the spring of hope, it was the winter of despair, we had everything before us, we had nothing before us, we were all going to heaven, we were all going direct the other way – in short, the period was so far like the present period, that some of its noisiest authorities insisted on its being received, for good or evil, in the superlative degree of comparison only.

One-Minute Prose Warm-Up

Newland Archer, during this brief episode, had been thrown into a strange state of embarrassment. It was annoying that the box which was thus attracting the undivided attention of masculine New York should be that in which his betrothed was seated between her mother and her aunt; and for a moment he could not identify the lady in the Empire dress, nor imagine why her presence created such excitement among the initiated. Then the light dawned on him, and with it came a momentary rush of indignation. No, indeed; no one would have thought the Mingotts would have tried it on! But they had; they undoubtedly had; for the low-toned comments behind him left no doubt in Archer's mind that the young woman was May Welland's cousin, the cousin always referred to in the family as "poor Ellen Olenska."

PART FIVE: On-Site Warm-Ups

Thirty-Second Warm-Up—Opening Your Body in All Directions

- Stand with your feet in a wide stance. Think your Alexander thoughts.
- Stretch your arms out to the sides, at shoulder height.
- Release your arms down.

- Stretch them a second time to the side.
- Whisper "ah." A nice open sound.
- Release your arms down.
- Stretch your arms up to the ceiling.
- Come up onto your toes.
- Whisper "ah." Open sound.
- Stay on your toes. Whisper "ah" a second time.
- Come back to center.
- Hum on your center pitch.

Thirty-Second Warm-Up—Cross-Pattern Stretch

- Stand comfortably. Think up.
- Kneel down or squat.
- Come onto the floor on all fours.
- Have your hands under your shoulders, and your knees under your hips.
- Your neck is free, your head balanced. Look at the floor.
- Leave your body long.
- Lift your right arm off the floor, stretch it straight in front of you, in line with your shoulder.
- Lift your left leg off the floor, stretch it straight out in back of you, in line with your hip.
- Your neck and back stay elongated. Whisper "ah."
- Bring your arm and leg down. Bring your left arm and right leg out. Whisper "ah."
- Come back to all fours. Feel how long you are.
- Return to a standing position.
- Whisper "ah."

Forty-Five-Second Warm-Up—Squatting

- Stand with your feet in a wide stance.
- Take hold of a makeup table that's attached to the wall, or a sink.
- Think up, and stay elongated as you lean slightly back.

- Let yourself come down into a squat.
- This will gently stretch your whole back, and your arms.
- Breathe out easily a few times.
- Allow your whole body to straighten and widen, as well as stretch.
- When it's time to come up, check to make sure you don't lift yourself up by tightening your shoulders, throwing your head back, or overusing your biceps.
- Lean back slightly, and push down through your feet.
- Momentum and your thigh muscles will bring you back up.
- Blow out the candle.

Forty-Five-Second Warm-Up—Child's Pose

- Stand at your full height.
- Thinking up, squat down to the floor.
- Alternatively, kneel down on the floor.
- Sit on your haunches.
- Let your torso drape forward over your knees. Your arms are stretched out above your head along the ground.
- This position of being folded forward on your folded up legs gently stretches your whole back, especially your lower back.
- Your arms are gently stretched, and your underarms and shoulders are opened.
- Your neck is free, and your head balanced, and supported, your forehead against the floor.
- When you are finished, you come back onto your haunches.
- Then come into a kneeling position, and back up into standing.

Forty-Five-Second Warm-Up—Wall Bend

- Stand with your back against the wall, your feet about nine inches away from the wall.
- Think up through your torso. Sense the support of the wall against your back.
- The back of your head won't be against the wall. (To do that you would collapse your head back and down.)

- There will be some curve in your lower back. You don't need to manipulate and flatten your back against the wall.
- Continue to think up, as you bend your knees forward.
- Your body will slide down the wall. It's similar to monkey, but without leaning forward. Take your time. It's a slow, controlled movement.
- Stop. Let yourself be in a bent position. Allow your lower back to release (again, don't try to flatten it), breathe easily, then slide up the wall.
- Repeat twice.

Color Warm-Up

This exercise is a way of dealing with the energy in your body in a tangible way. People who see you while you're doing the exercise won't be aware of what you're thinking or what you're working on, but they definitely know that you are focused. If you choose to work on this in an audition, just move as you would naturally, but imagine the color you're leaving everywhere. It gives you charisma, not through doing anything deliberately but through a quiet attraction that comes through the work.

- Bring yourself to a sense of quiet.
- Stay with a calm and centered place.
- Be aware of your mind-body-breath as you think your flow thoughts.
- Imagine that your body is very light and hollow.
- In your mind's eye, fill your body with air.
- Imagine the air moving around inside your body.
- Choose one of your favorite colors.
- Allow the color to fill up the inside of your whole body.
- Imagine the color is moving around with the air.
- Now begin to move. Start with your hands and arms. As you move, imagine that you leave streaks of color when you move your hands
- Begin to walk, moving your hands and arms.
- You leave trails of color wherever you move.
- Your energy begins to fill up the space all around you with the color.
- Imagine you fill the whole room with your energy, your color.

Thanksgiving Day Balloon

This is a creative and effective way to fill yourself with the energy of the character you will be playing. It's also a way you can expand your energy out in all directions without being pushy about it—it's coming organically from the inside. And it's fun.

- Center yourself through the flow concepts: *Neck free, head forward and up...*
- In your mind's eye imagine the Thanksgiving Day balloons you've seen. Giant balloons that float high above the street.
- Choose a favorite balloon, or imagine a balloon you'd like to see of an animal, a character, person, or something abstract.
- Imagine the balloon, deflated, lying on the ground. It takes many people to help inflate the balloon since it's so large.
- Let yourself become the balloon.
- Think about yourself slowly, gradually being filled with air.
- See yourself slowly filling up.
- Once you are full, begin to move, to walk, knowing that you are being taken along by the air inside of you.
- You don't need to push or force anything. You follow the energy that is inside you. In a way, you follow the energy that is leading you forward.

PART SIX: Cooldowns

Letting Go

Letting go after a performance can be a challenge, especially if it was a very exciting or difficult performance. Some actors are keyed up for hours afterward, and the tension lingers on in their bodies. There can almost be a feeling of a "high" after performing in a play. That's great for a short period, but it's not so great if that continues for hours and disrupts your rest and sleep. The same goes for a long day on a film set. Go through this process to bring yourself back to "neutral," so that you can rest and restore for the next day's work.

- Greet guests after the performance, if you have them.
- Take your time putting away your things and taking off your makeup.
- Be methodical rather than rushing.
- Put all your belongings in one place so you can conveniently pick them up when you're ready to leave the theater.
- Once you've finished that, sit quietly for a few moments.
- Allow your eyes to close.
- Remember whatever you felt went well in that day's performance.
- Make note of whatever you might change. You can write down these things in your mind-body journal.
- Give two sighs.
- Allow your whole body to free itself.
- Consciously begin to allow yourself to let go of the performance.
- Visualize the character you just played draining out of your body, as water drains out of a bathtub.
- Start at your head and work down through your whole body, allowing the character to leave.
- Now imagine that your body is filling up with air or with helium.
- You'll begin to feel lighter. The events of the play and the evening will begin to fade.
- Let yourself progressively leave the imaginary world of the play behind, and let your actual life begin to take over again.
- Give three whispered "ah"s, allowing your whole body to release and let go.
- Let your eyes open.
- By this time, you will be mostly "yourself," with only remnants of the character left behind.
- Consciously give yourself permission to let the character go. Trust that she will be there again when you need her. You don't need to hold onto her over the next twenty-four hours.

Preparing for Sleep

- Make your preparations for the next day. You might write a list of things to do so you're not mentally reminding yourself of things as you fall asleep.
- Prepare yourself for bed. Set your alarm(s).
- You may want to have soft music on. Something you find soothing.
- Get into bed. Rather than doing a reverse sit-up, slide down onto your side and roll onto your back. This keeps things easier in your neck and shoulders.
- Lie on your back, even if you don't sleep on your back.

- Have a pillow under your head, and bend your knees. Or put a pillow under each knee.
- Give two sighs.
- Remind yourself that your work is over for the day. You don't want to bring your character into your night's sleep. It's okay to let her go for now. She will be there in the morning.
- Think through *Let my neck be free, let my head be poised on the top of my spine, let my back lengthen and widen.*
- Do three blowing out the candles. Take a brief pause, then do three whispered "ah"s.
- Imagine that any tension that has built up over the day is slowly draining out of your body, as water drains out of a bathtub.
- Allow your body to feel both light and supported by the bed. You no longer need to support yourself. You can afford to fully let go.
- Let yourself release your body, your breath, and your cares.
- Trust. You can let go of your mind as well as your body. Your tidal breathing will rock you gently, almost like a mother rocking a baby in a crib. Trust. You will have a good night's sleep and you will wake rested and refreshed in the morning.

11

Your Psycho-Physical Health and Choice

Performers are usually "called" to their profession. It's a vocation, not just a job. There are so many other careers that are steadier, more predictable, and more "acceptable" to the general public. In fact, people who know very little about what it takes to actually live a life in the arts will tend to group performers on either of two ends of the spectrum of success: so-called starving artists or superstars. Audiences can be somewhat patronizing toward "starving artists," whom they appear both somewhat envious of (because of their rejection of the status quo) and somewhat patronizing toward ("Exactly how often are you working?" "How much money are you making doing that?"). The "superstars" are performers who have "made it"—whatever that may mean. Audiences are fascinated by this type of performer, wanting to know all about their personal lives and habits, their romantic lives, how much money they earn, and so on. Sometimes they exalt this type of actor to almost superhuman status, and if the performer comes into a difficult patch in their personal or professional life, there is often a sense of schadenfreude (pleasure that comes from someone else's misfortune).

But the average person has no conception of the life of the day-to-day professional working actor. This performer is usually neither starving in a garret nor speeding around with her entourage in a diamond-encrusted sports car. The professional actor is just that—a serious-minded individual working hard at her craft and her job. The audience would be surprised at just how hardworking this type of performer is. Her life is filled with going to auditions, callbacks, classes, meetings with agents and managers, working out, going to rehearsals, previews, and performances. The discipline of this life would seem exhausting and boring to people who are usually only aware of the glittery result of a polished performance.

Sometimes people make the assumption that if they haven't heard of you, you aren't doing well as an actor. This is interesting, because people don't make the same assumption about accountants, for instance. Also, audiences may not have heard of some of the highly gifted actors from fifty years ago, but that does not diminish those actors' accomplishments. As far as I'm concerned, "making it" is not necessarily limited to appearing on a major television show or in a blockbuster film. Though those are both very good accomplishments, a successful career in the arts means carving out a life for yourself that fulfills what you need it to be: creative, explorative, challenging, exciting, life-enhancing, and rewarding. I bring up this topic mostly as a reminder to stay on the path that works for you. It's best not to judge your life by others' standards but to mold a personal and professional life that is right for you. That way happiness lies.

For a successful life in the performing arts (and by "successful," I mean successful on your own terms), four things are imperative:

- Adaptability
- Ingenuity
- Transformational ability
- Authenticity

You can find all these things within yourself through what I term an *open receptive state*. When you are in this state, you are leaving yourself open to new experience, new possibilities, new choices.

The three important components of the Alexander Technique—sense, poise, flow—lead you to the final Alexander concept: *choice*. So often in our lives it feels like we have no choice. At other times, ironically, it may feel like there are a bewildering array of choices. The idea that you can control everything rigidly through your old habits and ways of being is false. If you can live out the concept of sense-poise-flow to the best of your ability, this gives you a very powerful life tool, one that you can use every day to guide yourself in your own life. I don't have to tell you how complex life is—how many scenarios it offers up, dilemmas, and even crises at times. But you have the ability to adapt yourself successfully to constantly changing circumstances and use your most powerful human capacity: to make a choice.

When you follow the Alexander precepts, you can employ what I call *constructive self-management* (Alexander called it constructive conscious control). It's one of the greatest tools you have. When you use it well, you're able to view yourself as objectively as possible, without judging yourself. You give up pushing for immediate results and grasping for "perfection" and pay attention to your process. Your commitment to process allows for continual growth, which gives full rein your artistry. When you stick with process-oriented approach, it's hard to put a foot wrong. Even when you make a "mistake," it's a powerful learning experience as opposed to a "defeat." This attitude of the possibility of change through your own constructive self-management can be a major shift in your personal life and a revolutionary one in your professional life. Being free from the restrictions and domination of your habits can become your "new normal."

One of the most effective strategies I've seen, both for self-acceptance and for being able to make the positive choices you want and need, is giving yourself the gift of time. Rather than rushing through everything, you can take whatever time you need. That's an irreplaceable gift, one you won't regret giving yourself. Because it takes time to change.

Habit is strong. It often gets in your way. You have tried-and-true ways of doing things, and stiff muscles, tension, tight movement, self-limiting thinking, and even pain can sometimes be the result. But on an unconscious level, your ways of functioning are something you at least know and to some degree are comfortable with. If you change, who knows what that would lead to? But if you look at the physical, mental, and emotional things that every actor would like mastery over, such as

- Your mind
- Your breathing
- Your body
- Your voice
- Your emotions

and if you organize the development of these parts of yourself into *small, doable steps*, as we have done in this book, you will be able to take that first step. And you'll be able to sustain the change. That first small step will lead you to the next. And the next. This holds true for physical tensions as well as how you plan your whole professional life in the performing arts.

Here's an example: Someone offers you the choice between a small but possibly attention-grabbing role in a big film (for a respectable fee), and at the same time you are offered a starring role in a prestigious off-Broadway play (at a small salary) that has a chance of moving to Broadway—but there's no guarantee it will move. What should you do? Your agent tells you to take the film, and your acting buddies, whom you trust, tell you to take the play. Which do you choose? If you give into your fear reactions, you'll probably do what you've always done, because that feels safest—even if your fear takes you in a direction you don't think is best for you in this professional situation.

Ideally, none of us should be prisoners of our own fear. That doesn't mean you'll never feel fear—you will. It's part of the human experience. But your fear doesn't have to overcome you, rule you, and determine your course in your artistic ambitions.

Even to consider your fear and its effect on your psycho-physical health is a great beginning. People acknowledge, hurriedly and in passing, that the mind and the body are connected. To some, it's almost an annoyance. Often they want the body to do what they want, when they want, without it getting tired or injured or having any problems at all. They want it separate in function from the mind, operating almost as a kind of servant. In essence, there is almost a disrespect for their own bodies. When the body gets weak or injured, people can be filled with a kind of fear, irritation, or indignation. "How can I be sick?" "Why can't I get better faster?" "Why does this always happen to me?" The answer is because the body has its own time. But we can help our bodies along, through good use of it, getting rest, having patience, and taking care of ourselves.

There's an apt expression: "If you don't live in your body, where are you going to live?" But many of us don't. We tend to get locked into our heads, or our imaginations. As actors, we need access to all three. Recognizing the importance of your body is primary. It's who you are, it's where you live, it *houses and embodies* your mind and imagination.

All your life experience is imprinted on your mind, heart, and body. Your body is the blueprint of your emotional experiences. Your experience is inside of you. That's why you never have to force or push in your acting—it's all there inside you. Learn to trust that it's there, whenever you need it. The more you can release in your mind, body, and breathing, the more you will facilitate the release of your emotions. It's simply a matter of *allowing it to happen*.

In your quest to become the best actor you can be, it's necessary for you to define for yourself what a healthy lifestyle is. How do you want to best use your time, fitting in all the things that are important to you personally and professionally? It's also vital to pinpoint what your personal stressors are, to understand what makes you feel most anxious or stressed. Auditions? Rehearsals? Directors you don't know? Agents and casting directors? The thought that you might not get another acting job? And what are the personal issues that make you most tense? Confrontations? Disagreements with family and close friends? Not knowing where you want to live? Unsure if you want to have children? It's important to think these issues through thoroughly, and perhaps write in your mind-body journal about it.

In addition, each of us seems to have an Achilles' heel or two. I know that, in the past, my lower back would tighten up when I felt under pressure—that's where my stress would go. It will be extremely useful for you to learn where your "heels" are: neck, shoulders, lower back? When you feel tightness and restriction there, this is not all negative. It's your body speaking to you, saying, "Hey. We've gotten a little off course here. Anything you can do to get us back on?"

A critical piece of the puzzle is acknowledging and honoring the things you do well and that are going well for you in your life and work. This will bring your stress levels down. Research shows that the old-fashioned concept of counting your blessings will help calm you: your mind, muscles, nervous system, and emotions. Peace of mind will help you find peace in your body. It also works the other way around.

A pragmatic thing you can do for yourself is to make a *mind-body plan* for the week or the month—five-, ten-, and fifteen-minute windows of time that you schedule for yourself to work on your use, your breathing, voice, movement, and mind-body unity. It's one of the most worthwhile things you can ever do for yourself. It's like the financial planners who tell you to start saving for a rainy day and retirement at age eighteen. Then you're supposed to continue to put some money away throughout the year, every year, because of the power of *compounding*. At the end of your life, you're left with more than enough money. It's the same principle working with yourself psycho-physically. Work on yourself a little bit every day and the results will compound greatly over time.

In committing to yourself and your goals, you will activate your talent and blossom into your full artistic expression. Undoing and letting go of what you don't need allows you to take flight. Then you can find mental-physical grace. In this way you can embody Stanislavski's definition of what acting is: "solitude in public" and "living truthfully under imaginary circumstances."

Acceptance of and respect for your own essence will help you allow it to be seen in your work. Staying truthful to your acting process will help you take your rightful place. You'll fill up your space by allowing yourself to expand mentally, physically, emotionally, vocally, and spiritually. The following quotation (often attributed to Ralph Waldo Emerson, but its true authorship is disputed) is inspirational for every actor:

> Whatever you do, you need courage. Whatever course you decide upon, there is always someone to tell you that you are wrong. There are always difficulties arising that tempt you to believe your critics are right. To map out a course of action and follow it to an end requires some of the same courage that a soldier needs. Peace has its victories, but it takes brave men and women to win them.

Step, Repeat

The red carpet tradition was supposedly invented by the famous English beauty Lillie Langtry. In the nineteenth century, actresses were responsible for providing their own costumes. Langtry wore beautiful, expensive gowns in her plays. Often the theaters she played in were filthy, so she had a red carpet laid from her dressing room to the stage to protect the white hems of her floor-length gowns. Now the red carpet is standard at Broadway openings and film festivals. Even small film festivals have several yards of red and a backdrop with their festival's logo. So it's quite likely that at some point you will "walk the red carpet." In Hollywood they call this the Step, Repeat. That means you walk into position on the red carpet, have your photograph taken, take another step or two, and have your photo taken again. At Cannes they say it can almost be frightening; there are hordes of people and a deafening roar. It can be challenging to keep your poise. At a very small festival, it may just be you and one photographer. Whether it's either of those extremes or something in between, the principle is the same: let yourself be yourself. Don't shrink from it—embrace it. Your work on the film is done: now is your chance to enjoy the fruits of your labor and the acknowledgment that comes with it.

- If you're wearing a coat or carrying bags, put them to the side in a pile, away from the cameras.
- If you need it, take a drink of water before you start, in case your mouth gets dry.
- Check quickly in a mirror to see that you look the way you want to look.
- Then forget the way you look.
- You may be with others from your play or film, or you may be on your own.
- Remember to let go of your neck, shoulders, and back.
- Soften your face.
- Take a breath or two.
- Remember to allow yourself to let go into your fullest height. (*Neck free, head forward up, torso lengthening and widening.*)
- Let your energy release up and out.
- Step onto the red carpet.
- Be aware of your body.
- And aware of the carpet beneath your feet.
- Aware of the space on either side of you, above you, and behind you. In front of you, too.
- Keep breathing easily.
- You might consider smiling. (Unless you're the smoldering type.)
- Walk into your first position.
- Stay in your body. Keep breathing.
- Face the camera.
- Look into the lens.

- Let yourself be seen.
- *Allow your essence to be seen.*
- Smile.
- Step.
- Repeat.

Textual References

Page 1
"For as long as I can remember..."
From acceptance speech for Screen Actors Guild Award for Outstanding
    Performance by a Male Actor in a Leading Role (*There Will Be Blood*), Daniel
    Day-Lewis, January 27, 2008.

Page 136
"It's all I have to bring today..."
"It's all I have to bring today (26)" by Emily Dickinson, in *The Poems of Emily
    Dickinson*, edited by Thomas H. Johnson (Cambridge, Mass.: The Belknap
    Press of Harvard University Press, 1955).

Page 137
Shall I compare thee to a summer's day...
From Sonnet 18 by William Shakespeare, in *The Riverside Shakespeare* (Boston:
    Houghton Mifflin Company, 1974), page 1752.

Page 139
"She walks in beauty..."
From "She Walks in Beauty" by George Gordon, Lord Byron, in *The Norton
    Anthology of Poetry*, 3rd edition (New York: W. W. Norton & Co., Inc., 1970),
    page 589.
"Some have won a wild delight..."
From "Passion" by Charlotte Brontë, in *Poems by Currer, Ellis, and Acton Bell* by
    Charlotte, Emily, and Anne Brontë (London: Smith, Elder & Co., 1846), page 112.
"Beds to the front of them..."
From "Beds to the Front of Them" by Louisa May Alcott, in *Hospital Sketches* by
    Louisa May Alcott (Boston: James Redpath, Publisher, 1863).
"In Xanadu did Kubla Khan..."
From "Kubla Khan" by Samuel Taylor Coleridge, in *The Norton Anthology of
    Poetry*, 3rd edition (New York: W. W. Norton & Co., Inc., 1970), page 564.
"The shell of objects inwardly consumed..."
From "My Last Dance" by Julia Ward Howe, in *Passion-flowers* by Julia Ward
    Howe (Boston: Ticknor, Reed, and Fields, 1854), page 108.
"What was he doing, the great god Pan..."
From "A Musical Instrument" by Elizabeth Barrett Browning, in *The Norton
    Anthology of Poetry*, 3rd edition (New York: W. W. Norton & Co., Inc., 1970),
    page 675.

"Four seasons fill the Measure of the year..."
From "The Human Seasons" by John Keats, in *Selected Poems and Letters*
  by John Keats, edited by Douglas Bush (Boston: Houghton Mifflin
  Company, 1959), page 137.

Page 159
"Over hill, over dale..."
From "A Midsummer Night's Dream" by William Shakespeare, Act 2, Scene 1,
  in *The Riverside Shakespeare* (Boston: Houghton Mifflin Company, 1974),
  page 226.

Page 159
"When the night wind howls..."
From *Ruddigore, or The Witch's Curse* by W. S. Gilbert (London: G. Bell & Sons,
  Ltd., 1912), page 150.
"Life, believe, is not a dream..."
From "Life" by Charlotte Brontë, in *Poems by Currer, Ellis, and Acton Bell*
  by Charlotte, Emily, and Anne Brontë (London: Smith, Elder & Co., 1846),
  page 81.

Page 160
"Let me begin with facts..."
From *Dracula* by Bram Stoker (London: Penguin Classics, 2003), page 37.
"It was the best of times..."
From *A Tale of Two Cities* by Charles Dickens (London: James Nisbet &
  Co., Ltd., 1902), page 3.
"Newland Archer..."
From *The Age of Innocence* by Edith Wharton, chapter 2 (New York: Signet
  Classics, 1962), page 19.

Acknowledgments

My heartfelt thanks for their expertise, guidance, support, and fellowship: Bloomsbury Methuen Drama; my agent, Barbara Clark; my publisher, Jenny Ridout; my editor, John O'Donovan; my designer, Catherine Wood; my copy editor, Vinod Kumar; my project manager, Avinash Singh; and Lauren Schiff for pointing the way.

My Alexander teachers:
Judith Leibowitz, Barbara Kent, Glynn MacDonald, Debby Caplan, Pearl Ausubel, Sarnell Ogus, Pamela Anderson, Troup and Ann Matthews, Walter and Dilys Carrington, Marjorie Barstow, June Ekman, Beret Arcaya, and John Nicholls.

My Alexander colleagues:
Joan Frost, Cynthia Knapp, Teva Bjerken, Cynthia Reynolds, Thomas Vasiliades, Joan Arnold, Judith Stern, Jane Kosminsky, Carolyn Monka Serota, Jaye Dougherty, Kim Jessor, Gwen Ellison, Jean-Louis Rodrigue, Pamela Blanc, Frank Ottiwell, Amy Pell, Eleanor Rosenthal, Nancy Wanich Romita, Daniel Singer, Anne Holmes Waxman, Ralph Zito, Anne Rodiger, Belinda Mello, Meade Andrews, Sarah Barker, Evangeline Benedetti, Morgan Rysdon, Joanne Howell, Nadia Banna, and Nanette Walsh.

My classical music colleagues:
Ruth Falcon, Ruth Golden, Gary Schocker, Arthur Levy, Amy Burton, Sherry Overholt, Beth Roberts, Linda Pierce Hunter, Connie Barnett, LeAnn Overton, Joan Krueger, and Eve Gigliotti.

My medical and mind-body wellness colleagues:
Andrea Wolkenberg, PT, Gail King, PT, Dr. Jack Stern, Dr. Alexander Simotas, Dr. Howard Rosner, Dr. John Austin, Dr. Bradley Cash, Dr. Frances Halberg, Dr. Corrie Horshinski, Dr. Lucy Brown, Dr. Er Ke Yu, Amy Lemen, LCSW, Caroline Kohles, and everyone at the Jewish Community Center in Manhattan.

My family, friends, students and colleagues:
Nancy Connington, Melissa Glueck, Deirdre Broderick, Liz, Jeff, Allie, Sarah, Joe and Mary Alice Pojanowski, Michael Cooper, Asa Hoffman, Thomas Caruso,

Kelley Van Dilla, Rebecca Alford, Dr. Gordon LeGrand, Dan Cordle, AnnMarie Benedict and Jeff Pagliano, Julie and Joe Donato, Shelagh Carter, Barbara Sher, Susan and Betsy Adams, Cheryl and Victor Houser, Colin Sutherland, Elaine Moran and Mark Glassman, Willow Johnson, Michael Milton, Joan Rosenfels, Karen Braga, Rudy and Elaine Schott, Jenny Cline, Oliver Houser, Chris and Casey Silva, Erin Sax, Brad Cole, Cora Rosevear, Mildred and Naomi Moskowitz, Susan Leslie, Mark Barlett, Pat Vega, and James Lipton, Walton Wilson, of Yale Drama School.

Institutions:
Yale Drama School, the Juilliard School, New York University's Tisch School of the Arts, the Actors Studio Drama School, the London Academy of Music and Dramatic Art, the American Academy of Dramatic Art, the Alvin Ailey School, American Center for the Alexander Technique, American Society for the Alexander Technique, Society of Teachers of the Alexander Technique, the New York International Fringe Festival, Theatre Row, the Gerald W. Lynch Theater at John Jay College, the Cleveland Film Festival, the Williamsburg Film Festival, the Boston International Film Festival, the Edmond J. Safra Parkinson's Wellness Program at NYU Langone Medical Center and JCC Manhattan, Spine Options, Opera America, Mannes School of Music, Westchester Summer Vocal Institute, the National Society of Colonial Dames in the State of New York, Van Cortlandt House, New York Society Library, Holy Cross Monastery, Mariandale Retreat Center, 92nd Street YMHA, the Jewish Community Center in Manhattan, West Side YMCA, and the Episcopal Actors Guild.

Special thanks to:
Jessica Wolf, for her reviewing, re-reviewing, counsel, support, and friendship.

Index

Exercise Videos

To view a particular video, please visit its URL below, or go to www.vimeo.com/channels/connington.

1   p. 17—Finding Where You Are: https://vimeo.com/81010082
2   pp. 18, 20—Coming Down onto and Up off the Floor: https://vimeo.com/84873587
3   p. 19—Constructive Rest: https://vimeo.com/84874095
4   p. 22—Mind-Body Opening: https://vimeo.com/84874096
5   p. 38—Postural Extremes: https://vimeo.com/84874233
6   p. 49—Critical Moment: https://vimeo.com/84874234
7   p. 51—Up Energy Through Your Whole Body: https://vimeo.com/84874235
8   p. 72—The Daily Tune-In: https://vimeo.com/84874626
9   p. 73—Sitting at the Computer: https://vimeo.com/84874236
10   p. 76—Walking: https://vimeo.com/84874237
11   p. 77—Moving In and Out of a Chair: https://vimeo.com/84874723
12   p. 95—Blowing Out the Candle: https://vimeo.com/84874725
13   p. 97—Whispered "Ah" and Counting: https://vimeo.com/84874724
14   p. 156—Three-Minute Warm-Up: https://vimeo.com/84874726

Contact

To invite Bill Connington to teach seminars, workshops, or classes, or to visit your college, university, or school, please contact him at

billconnington@gmail.com

Visit his website:

http://www.createabalance.org/

Follow him on Twitter: @BillConnington1

Find him on Facebook: www.facebook.com/bill.connington

Find him on Instagram: billconnington

Bill also contributes a blog to Actors & Performers.

Please visit www.actorsandperformers.com